BACKYARD
IDEA BOOK

BACKYARD
IDEA BOOK

LEE ANNE WHITE

The Taunton Press

For Alan, with love

The Taunton Press
Inspiration for hands-on living®

The Taunton Press, Inc., 63 South Main Street, PO Box 5506, Newtown, CT 06470-5506
e-mail: tp@taunton.com

EDITOR: Marilyn Zelinsky Syarto
JACKET/COVER DESIGN: Jeannet Leendertse
INTERIOR DESIGN: Lori Wendin
LAYOUT: Laura Lind Design
ILLUSTRATOR: Christine Erikson
FRONT COVER PHOTOGRAPHERS: Top row, left to right: © Alan & Linda Detrick; © Robert Stein;
© Alan & Linda Detrick; © Lee Anne White.
Middle row, left to right: © Tim Street-Porter; © Robert Stein; © Brian Vanden Brink, Photographer 2004.
Bottom row, left to right: © Lee Anne White, © Eric Roth, © Anne Gummerson Photography,
© Lee Anne White
BACK COVER PHOTOGRAPHERS: Top: © Brian Vanden Brink, Photographer 2004;
Bottom left and center: © Lee Anne White; bottom right: © Tim Street-Porter

Library of Congress Cataloging-in-Publication Data
White, Lee Anne.
  Backyard idea book / Lee Anne White.
     p. cm.
  ISBN-13: 978-1-56158-667-7
  ISBN-10: 1-56158-667-6
  1. Backyard gardens. 2. Garden ornaments and furniture. I. Title.
  SB473.W49 2004
  717--dc22
                              2004009747

Printed in the United States of America
10 9 8 7

Acknowledgments

Writing a book is often viewed as a solitary task. And often, it does begin to feel that way. But pulling together an idea book is a wonderfully collaborative experience, and I have many to thank for their creativity, advice, support, and encouragement.

Most importantly, I'd like to acknowledge the many photographers who contributed images; the landscape architects, architects, landscape designers, interior designers, and garden designers who created these spaces; and the homeowners who have so graciously shared their backyards with us. They are listed individually in the credits for this book.

On a more personal note, there are those who consented to interviews, answered questions, helped arrange photo shoots, shared plans of their projects, or contributed to my education as a designer. Their thoughts, ideas, and advice are woven throughout this book. To Barbara Allen, Betty Ajay, Barbara Blossom Ashmun, Jeff Bale, Margaret de Haas van Dorsser, Michelle Derviss, Tracy DiSabato-Aust, Kevin Doyle, Sydney Eddison, David Ellis, Brooks Garcia, Keith Geller, Erica Glasener, Nancy Goodwin, John Harper, Gary Keim, Ann Lovejoy, Anna Kondolf, Brad McGill, David Bennett McMullin, Richard McPherson, Keeyla Meadows, Carrie Nimmer, Carole Ottesen, Paula Refi, Doug Ruhren, Warren Simmonds, Andrew Schulman, David Schwartz, Isis Spinola-Schwartz, Michael Thilgen, and David Thorne, I offer my deepest gratitude. To landscape architect Jeni Webber, who has been so generous with her knowledge and experience and is never more than a phone call away, I am especially grateful.

Several organizations were particularly helpful in providing information regarding trends, safety issues, construction, and new products. Many thanks to the Hearth, Patio & Barbecue Association, the National Spa & Pool Institute, Master Pool Builders Association, Laneventure, Frontgate, *Fine Gardening,* and *Fine Homebuilding.*

A special note of appreciation goes to the editors, art directors, production staff, and marketing group at The Taunton Press who helped make this book possible—especially managing editor Carolyn Mandarano, editor Marilyn Zelinsky Syarto, and editorial assistants Robyn Doyon-Aitken and Jenny Peters. You have all been a pleasure to work with.

Contents

Introduction

It may not be obvious as you drive down the street, but there's a minor revolution taking place in America's backyards. Behind those picket fences, we are retreating to the backyard after long work weeks and relaxing on our decks, porches, and patios. We're fleeing the comfort of air-conditioned interiors to cook, dine, and entertain alfresco. We're escaping to backyard playgrounds, courts, and pools for hours of family fun and games. Now that we've rediscovered the joys of staying at home, we're finding new ways to spend that time outdoors.

This shift toward outdoor living is changing the way we design backyards. Large expanses of green grass are surrendering to smaller patches of more easily managed lawn. Long, regimented rows of

vegetables are being replaced by small yet efficient kitchen gardens planted just outside the back door. Folding chairs on concrete surfaces are being deserted for cushioned sofas on flagstone patios and redwood decks, often flanked by cozy fireplaces, outdoor kitchens, and soothing water features. The lines between indoors and out are forever blurred.

Our concept of backyard activities is expanding, too. Swings may never lose their attraction, but they are just one element in a backyard playground that also includes slides, forts, bridges, and climbing structures. Badminton nets and croquet hoops are still common, but so are bike paths, bocce courts, and putting greens. And swimming pools—once little more than rectangular holes in the ground—now run the gamut from pint-sized plunge pools and long, narrow lap

pools to naturalistic pools with boulders, beaches, and waterfalls.

In *Backyard Idea Book*, you'll get a look at the latest trends in outdoor design to help you sort through the many new products and innovative ideas designed for outdoor living. And you'll find inspiration for enhancing your own backyard with inviting spaces in which you'll want to spend many sunny afternoons and starry evenings while relaxing among family and friends.

The Inviting Backyard

Backyards are no longer just large expanses of lawn. They increasingly encompass a wide range of inviting spaces designed for recreation and relaxation.

At the heart of this transition is our desire to spend more time at home with family and friends and to make the most of the space we have—both indoors and out. While fresh air compels us to head outside, technology also plays a key role in our ability to spend more time outdoors. Advances in outdoor lighting make backyards more accessible and inviting after dark. New types of patio heaters and fireplaces comfortably extend the outdoor season. Designs for outdoor kitchens transform backyard barbecues into gourmet feasts. Construction innovations make pools and spas more affordable. And the development of durable, weather-resistant materials for furniture and fabrics continues to enhance the style and comfort of outdoor furnishings.

Successful backyard design, however, involves much more than adding appliances or accessories. It's best approached as part of the overall home-design process—one that addresses the relationship between indoor and outdoor spaces.

◀ START PLANNING A BACKYARD with simple, affordable, and creative ideas. This setting has all the ingredients of an inviting outdoor room: shade, a sense of enclosure, style, easy access to the kitchen, a view from the living room, and a place to eat, work, or converse.

EXPAND YOUR LIVING SPACE

A home's living space can be doubled by making the most of a backyard. After all, many backyards have a greater footprint than the house itself. And you can creatively transform even the tiniest of spaces into inviting outdoor rooms that beckon use in all but the coolest of seasons.

Inside our homes, there are rooms we gather in and rooms we escape to for relaxation. Outdoors, we need those same kinds of spaces. Porches, decks, patios, and pools make excellent gathering places. In fact, we can design multiple spaces for various types of get-togethers—perhaps a cozy patio for a romantic dinner, a comfortable deck for family meals, and a generous-sized terrace for hosting a crowd. When families entertain outdoors, it's ideal to have separate spaces for the parents to visit while the kids play with friends. Escapes can be as simple

▲ TERRACING INCREASES THE USABLE AREA in a sloped yard by creating two or more level surfaces for gathering spaces, play spaces, or gardens. The terracing in this backyard formed two gathering places, as well as opportunities for built-in seating and raised garden beds.

OUTDOOR LIVING AND RECREATIONAL SPACES

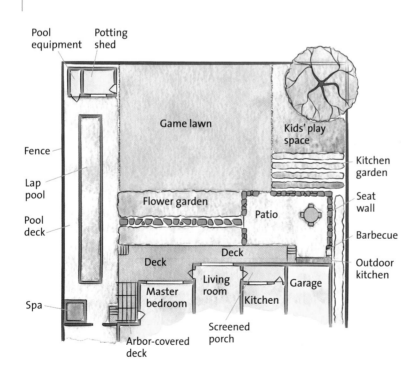

Pool equipment
Potting shed
Game lawn
Kids' play space
Fence
Kitchen garden
Lap pool
Flower garden
Patio
Seat wall
Pool deck
Barbecue
Deck
Deck
Living room
Garage
Outdoor kitchen
Master bedroom
Kitchen
Spa
Screened porch
Arbor-covered deck

as a hammock strung between two trees and a fort for young children or as elaborate as a freestanding studio for an artist and potting shed for an avid gardener.

The Indoor-Outdoor Connection

The most frequently used spaces are those that visually and physically bridge the gap between indoors and out. These spaces are seen through interior windows and doors. From outdoors, they connect to the house in the form of porches, decks, and patios. These intermediate—or transitional—spaces are among the most inviting because the house provides a sense of security and amenities are always nearby.

When porches, decks, and patios are planned as integral elements of a new or renovated home, they can be designed to

▶ RICH WOOD SURFACES, wool blankets, and a blazing fire lend a sense of warmth to this porch. Compared with the open deck at the end of the house, which offers enticing views of the lake, the covered and furnished porch provides an intimate gathering space.

◀ THIS OUTDOOR ROOM was created by an interior decorator who treated the patio as she would have a living room. Decorative accents adorn the wall and tables, chairs are arranged in conversational groupings, and brick warms the floor as a rug might indoors.

create indoor-outdoor transitions that are so subtle they blur the line where the house ends and the landscape begins. For continuity between spaces, construction materials should echo those of the house; decorating themes and colors can easily carry over outside from interior rooms.

These intermediate spaces should also relate in a functional way to adjacent rooms. For example, an outdoor dining area is most conveniently located just beyond the kitchen door. A larger outdoor space for entertaining should flow easily from a living room or family room. A secret-garden patio just large enough for two is ideally located outside a master bedroom.

Vary the Spaces

As you move farther away from the house, spaces tend to become more casual—sometimes relating more to the surrounding landscape than to the house. Throughout the yard, spaces should vary in shape, size, and character. Relaxing spaces, for instance, should feature comfortable chairs and lounges, while dining areas need sturdy tables and outdoor cooking amenities; both should be positioned for afternoon shade in hot climates. Children's play spaces require soft landing surfaces, while areas for entertaining large crowds call for

▲ A HAMMOCK in a secluded corner of the yard offers a place of quiet refuge after a long week. Be sure to hang a hammock between two trees or build a sturdy arbor, like this one, for support. In hot climates, remember to choose a shady spot.

▼ THE CAREFUL COORDINATION of materials between the living room and patio results in a near-seamless transition from indoors to outdoors. Matching floor tiles, modular design features, and metallic finishes pull the rooms together, while the large glass sliding doors eliminate any remaining visual barriers between the spaces.

smooth surfaces than can be easily negotiated in dim light or with drinks in hand. Design some areas for sitting or lounging, others for standing or strolling, and one or more for activity, especially if you have children.

CREATE YOUR OWN DOMAIN

Unlike many front yards, which are semi-public spaces shared with neighbors, backyards can be personal spaces where you are free to express your own sense of style and way of living. But even with more design options, you'll feel most comfortable with a little privacy built into your backyard.

△ THESE TWO MASSIVE MASONRY WALLS serve multiple purposes: They screen unwanted views of the neighbor's house, help define one side of the outdoor room, and add a striking focal point against the green landscape—much like a bright painting on a dark wall.

◄ ON SMALL LOTS, fences take up very little space and can be detailed with stylized posts, pickets, and gates to give a space character. The pickets in the weathered fence and white gate are spaced just wide enough to let in light and air without losing privacy.

For added privacy, wooden fences are quick, easy, and affordable to install. However, there are other ways to achieve seclusion. Masonry walls, hedges, mixed plantings, vine-covered trellises, and outbuildings also help enclose a backyard. Although the periphery of the backyard is the logical place for an enclosure, screening gathering spaces that are located close to the house makes them feel cozy and protected, while making the yard appear more expansive.

To create personal, private backyard domains, involve each member of the household in the planning process. Everyone will have different opinions and needs, but there's room in every backyard to include a special space or unique feature for all. (And don't forget that pets need their outdoor spaces, too.) Start by brainstorming or creating a wish list. Chances are, there will be more on the list than can be accomplished, but priorities will emerge as plans develop, and the backyard will begin to fall into shape.

START BY DIVIDING SPACES

Sometimes, the biggest challenge is just getting started. A tiny backyard plot can feel hopelessly limiting, while a large expanse of lawn can appear daunting. In each case, the best approach is to begin by dividing the space.

In tight spaces, it's important to make every inch count. A composition of several cozy areas has a way of feeling much larger than a single medium-sized space. And if there's not room to divide, simply laying out paths, patios, or lawns diagonally or along an S-curve makes a yard appear bigger by allowing it to unfold gradually

▲ THIS STUDIO and small, adjacent lawn are encircled by dense plantings, which lend privacy to the setting. A series of four double glass doors along one wall of the studio allow the room to be flooded with natural light.

rather than in a single glance. Paying close attention to details, such as paving materials or plant combinations, also makes a small space seem larger, as it takes longer to visually absorb all of the elements.

Division works on a larger scale, too. Divide expansive properties into smaller, functional spaces so they appear more inviting and manageable. When you are planning your backyard spaces, identify areas for cooking, dining, entertaining, gardening, swimming, or playing ball, and determine how much space is required for each. Also, be sure to define areas that you wish to leave in their natural state—such as meadows or woodland groves.

It takes time to implement the plans for an entire backyard, so tackle one area at a time, and don't be surprised if it takes a period of several years to finish the project. Start with areas closest to the house because you can see them from indoors and because they will be used most frequently. Also address any urgent outdoor needs up front—such as storage or play spaces for children.

▲ WITH A SPA, SWIMMING POOL, outdoor kitchen, large lawn, woods, and multiple seating areas, everyone in this family can be outdoors at the same time without feeling crowded. The pool is positioned for maximum sun exposure, while umbrellas provide shady areas to beat the heat.

DIVIDING BACKYARD SPACES

LARGE YARDS

Divide large yards into manageable, inviting spaces focused
on particular activities.

SMALL YARDS

Define areas in a small yard to create cozy yet functional spaces.

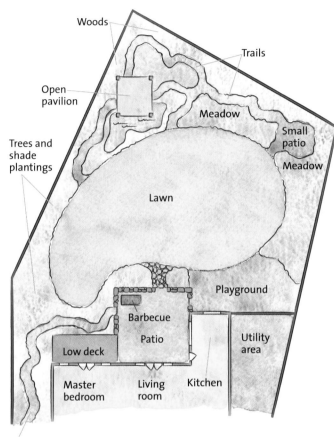

Woods

Trails

Open
pavilion

Meadow

Small
patio

Trees and
shade
plantings

Meadow

Lawn

Playground

Barbecue

Patio

Utility
area

Low deck

Master
bedroom

Living
room

Kitchen

Side yard access

Sunny
garden

Counter   Barbecue   Fence

Arbor

Brick
patio

Dining

Gate

Shady
border

Flagstone
patio

Potting
bench

Stoop shaded
with arbor

Compost
bin

House

◄ SEATING LEDGES built into these
walls allow the center of this
patio to be left open for entertaining larger crowds. The kids
have room to play, too, with a
large lawn adjacent to the home
playground equipment.

▲ WHEN SUBDIVIDING A YARD, individual areas can be defined with walls and fences or by simply changing the materials underfoot. Both strategies are used in this landscape, which includes a fence, pea-gravel garden paths, a flagstone patio, and a mulched area near the oyster-shell bocce-ball court along the periphery.

▲ THIS SMALL, URBAN BACKYARD in San Francisco features five separate areas, each located on a different level. In addition to the central courtyard, upper garden, and lower courtyard shown here, there is a sunken dining patio near the kitchen and a deck off the living room.

Define and Connect Spaces

Regardless of size, backyard spaces should be clearly defined and conveniently connected. This may be as simple as changing the paving materials when one space transitions into another—such as stepping from a flagstone patio onto a lawn. However, building a low seating wall around a patio or adding a step between two areas will distinguish the spaces from one another without taking away from the open feeling. To make spaces feel cozier, build 4-ft. to 6-ft.-high walls between them.

To avoid revealing a backyard all at once and to create inviting destinations, conceal distant spaces partially or entirely from view and prolong the experience of getting there—perhaps with a narrow path that meanders through a garden area. By varying the size of spaces and the degree to which they are open or enclosed, you can create a series of outdoor areas appropriate for numerous activities, for changing numbers of people, and for enjoying at different times of the day and night.

▲ THIS BACKYARD is less than 25 ft. deep, so the space was divided vertically—with decks extending from each level of the house—to create more livable space. As a result, everyone in the family can find a quiet place to escape.

COLLABORATE WITH NATURE

Nature is a great collaborator in the design process. By taking advantage of your backyard's existing natural features and considering the impact of your decisions on the greater landscape, you can create beautiful and healthy environments.

If you are creating a backyard from scratch while building a new house, preserving existing trees during construction will provide shade and screening, which will reduce a home's heating bills. When redesigning an existing backyard, opting for permeable surfaces, such as dry-laid stone, pea gravel, or mulch, will allow rainwater to soak into the ground rather than run off into drainage ditches. Choosing fuel-efficient outdoor grills and building patio

▲ WHO NEEDS A LAWN when you have woods? During construction, the builders were careful to leave as many trees surrounding this house as possible. With the stone, wood, and twig building materials, the house looks like it has emerged naturally from the surrounding landscape.

◄ LAWNS PLAY an important role in the landscape but require time and resources to keep them looking good. Make a strong visual statement by creating lawns only as large as needed and defining them with hedges, patios, or edging materials.

▲ UNCUT AREAS beyond the mown lawn reduce yard work, provide a home for animals, and create a stunning view. Meadows and broad swaths of tall grasses also make a natural transition between a kept yard and woodland buffer.

▼ THIS HOUSE is only blocks away from Atlanta's skyscrapers, but you'd never know it. By preserving the mature oaks, eliminating the lawn, and planting native shrubs and perennials, this backyard feels more like it's located on the side of a secluded mountain. With the addition of a pond, the entire environment provides an ideal habitat for birds.

floors or fences and decks with recycled or ecologically harvested materials conserve natural resources. Building low-emission outdoor fireplaces or choosing alternative fuels for fireplaces also helps protect the earth's ozone layer.

By replacing sections of lawn with mixed plantings, you can help restore lost habitats for birds, butterflies, and toads. A mix of native and well-adapted plants will reduce the need for supplementary water and fertilizer. All of this requires planning, but by planting with ecology in mind, you'll ultimately have more time to spend relaxing in your backyard.

Dining and Relaxing

When planning outdoor rooms, take design cues from your home's indoor
spaces. By designing a porch, patio, deck, pavilion, or casual seating area with
the same attention given to an indoor room, you can create a place to gather
with your family, to entertain friends, or to escape to after a long day at work.

An outdoor room can have a floor, walls, a ceiling, comfortable furnishings, and decorative
accents just like your living room, dining room, or kitchen. An exterior space may even be
similar to an indoor room in shape, size, and furniture arrangement. However, when deciding
what type of structures and furnishings to include in an outdoor room, keep in mind the
changing quality and amount of light, the fluctuating temperatures and weather patterns, the
sounds of nature and neighborhoods, and the life cycle of the landscape.

One or more areas designed for open-air living enhance any backyard. Start by positioning a gathering space—especially one designed for dining—close to the house for convenience. Add areas with comfortable seating in both the sun and shade, and provide a porch,
awning, or other structure for shelter from sudden rainstorms. Use walls, fences, or hedges
to increase privacy. Place plants adjacent to stone, brick, concrete, or wood to soften the
hard surfaces. Finally, use container plantings, water features, or outdoor sculpture to provide the finishing touches to an outdoor room.

◄ AS LONG AS THE WEATHER cooperates, an outdoor room can be just as inviting as an indoor room, especially
if it includes comfortable seating arranged to encourage casual conversation. Walls of greenery loosely enclose
the seating area in this backyard. A carpet of crushed gravel defines the space.

Under the Shelter of a Porch or Portico

ORCHES, PORTICOS, VERANDAS, LOGGIAS, AND BALCONIES are all sheltered outdoor spaces connected to a house. These in-between spaces are spots in which to enjoy fresh air and the surrounding landscape without leaving the comfort and security of home. Because it is sheltered, a covered room gets more use than other outdoor spaces, especially if it is tucked into a cozy nook or corner of the house for protection from prevailing winds. An outdoor fireplace makes a roofed space even cozier and more inviting during chilly evenings.

A screened porch keeps bugs at bay and increases privacy, while an open porch heightens the awareness of being outdoors. Because of its close proximity to the interior of a house, a porch is a place to begin and end each day, to serve meals, and for children's play, especially when appropriately furnished. Furnishings for a porch can be as simple as a couple of rocking chairs or as elaborate as a room full of sofas, tables, chests, rugs, and lamps, depending on what types of activities are planned for the space.

◄ THE VAULTED CEILING of this porch adds height and makes the space feel like it is open to the surrounding woods. Materials such as natural wood shingles and exposed beams blend the structure into the setting.

◄ KEEP BEAUTIFUL—or uninviting—views in mind when determining the location for a new porch. This porch looks out onto a stone patio and natural, woodland setting. While considering the scenery, remember that eastern views catch the sunrise and western views capture the sunset.

▼ BROAD STEPS THAT RUN THE WIDTH of the porch create an almost seamless flow of space between the interior, porch, and patio of this home. Placing the outdoor dining area on the covered porch makes it convenient to the kitchen.

▶ A SCREENED PORCH often doubles as a dining room in pleasant weather, expanding a home's living space. In moderate climates, a screened porch can be used nine months of the year. This porch's dining area has floor-to-ceiling screening to bring in more of the outdoors.

► BY PLACING SKYLIGHTS in a porch roof like this one, the sunlight brightens the porch and the adjacent interior room. In warm climates, an eastern exposure prevents the rooms from overheating in the afternoon. In cool climates, a southern exposure warms up the space during the day.

◄ MOST PORCHES ARE BUILT against one or more walls of a house. This porch, however, is separated from the house by a breezeway, allowing the porch to have screens on all four sides. In inclement weather, sliding doors drawn along two sides of the porch protect the space from wind and blowing rain.

Sprucing Up a Stoop

A STOOP OR LANDING—the area just beyond the back door—provides the "formal" connection between a house and the backyard. No matter how tiny a stoop might be, it should be a pleasant place to pass through or perhaps to pause for a few moments to sit on a bench or step to pet the dog or watch the setting sun.

▼THIS BACKDOOR STOOP was transformed into a small deck with steps wrapping around the corners. The deck has room for a couple of chairs, a simple bench, and container plantings. The arbor around the door helps frame the rear entry.

▲A CURVED, BRICK LANDING, a Spanish-style wood-and-tile over-hang, and a custom-designed contemporary screen door with color-ful matching trim give this small stoop character. A multicolored collection of pots and plants adds the finishing touch.

▶THIS SHALLOW BUT LONG SHELTERED ENTRY is enhanced with a built-in bench for seating. The bench provides a spot to pull off muddy boots before entering the house, visit with pets, or escape a sudden shower.

▶ A BREEZEWAY is a passageway, but it can also serve as a porchlike gathering space with the addition of a few comfortable chairs. This space catches the slightest breezes, but a ceiling fan adds character and keeps the air circulating on still days.

▼ A PORCH GETS LOTS OF TRAFFIC because it is a transitional area used to go in and out of a house. The rocking chairs on this back porch are invitations to pause and enjoy the view. A table and chairs tucked into the corner encourage a longer stay.

▼ PORCH SWINGS are traditionally hung with chains. This one is attached to the porch roof with marine-grade white rope, which blends in better with the surrounding coastal architecture and beach furniture. It also eliminates the squeaking associated with chains.

▶ INDOOR FURNITURE suits a multipurpose, all-weather porch. A game table quickly converts for dining. Casual chests, freestanding country closets, and bookcases store games, toys, table linens, and throws. A sofa doubles as an extra bed in warm weather.

▲ EXPOSED WOOD ON PORCH FLOORS takes a beating from sun, rain, and wind, so rot-resistant wood or composite decking material is essential. Pressure-treated pine, Douglas fir, cedar, redwood, mahogany, and tropical hardwoods all weather well and require minimal care.

Anatomy of an Outdoor Room

Though it's helpful to compare outdoor and indoor rooms during the backyard planning stage, the materials used to create each type of space differ. For example, outdoor flooring materials have to stand up to weather. Also, fewer surfaces are covered with solid, impervious materials. Here are ideas to help you create an indoor, roomlike setting outdoors.

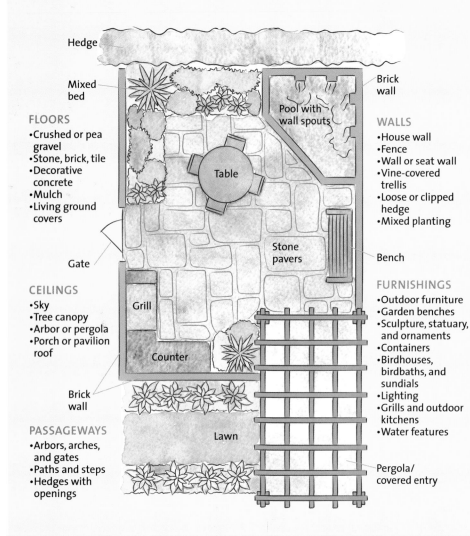

Hedge

Mixed bed

FLOORS
- Crushed or pea gravel
- Stone, brick, tile
- Decorative concrete
- Mulch
- Living ground covers

Gate

CEILINGS
- Sky
- Tree canopy
- Arbor or pergola
- Porch or pavilion roof

Brick wall

PASSAGEWAYS
- Arbors, arches, and gates
- Paths and steps
- Hedges with openings

Pool with wall spouts

Table

Stone pavers

Grill

Counter

Lawn

Brick wall

Pool with wall spouts

WALLS
- House wall
- Fence
- Wall or seat wall
- Vine-covered trellis
- Loose or clipped hedge
- Mixed planting

Bench

FURNISHINGS
- Outdoor furniture
- Garden benches
- Sculpture, statuary, and ornaments
- Containers
- Birdhouses, birdbaths, and sundials
- Lighting
- Grills and outdoor kitchens
- Water features

Pergola/ covered entry

▲ THE ARCHITECTURAL ELEMENTS of a house influence porch details. Here, custom railings with round posts and finials mimic an interior staircase and add a touch of elegance to the back porch. The closely spaced pickets safely enclose the area. The columns and railings are painted white to match the house trim, helping to tie the structure more closely to the house.

▶ A WRAPAROUND PORCH has room for a variety of sunny and shady spaces to suit different times of the day. This cozy seating area nestled in the corner of the porch is private so it won't be interrupted by passersby.

▲ A PORCH SHOULD MEASURE a minimum of 6 ft. wide. Anything narrower starts to feel cramped and out of scale with the house. An 8-ft. to 12-ft.-wide porch easily accommodates a hammock, a group of chairs, or a small dining table.

▶ THE WELL-DEFINED SEATING AREA on this back porch creates a room within a room. This sitting room is delineated by corner drapes, as well as by a narrowed passageway created by box planters. A light fixture is centered in the ceiling above the furniture.

◄ THIS PORCH is regularly used for relaxing and dining because it is adjacent to the kitchen. The high, vaulted roofline and custom railings give the porch character, while a skylight helps brighten the space.

▼ WOOD IS THE TRADITIONAL flooring for porches, but cut stone, flagstone, and tile are also appropriate weather-resistant materials. They are cool under-foot, making them ideal in warm climates or on porches with strong sun exposure.

▲ EVEN THOUGH THIS PORTICO receives ample natural light, light fixtures extend the hours of outdoor enjoyment, creating a space that can be used day or night. A chandelier provides ambient lighting, while a wall sconce increases visibility along one side. Uplights accent the palms to create a striking focal point in the corner.

▶ THE TILE FLOORING and seating area of this outdoor space extends beyond the roof of the portico to form a subtle transition between the house and landscape. A fireplace adds warmth on cool nights.

Warming Up an Outdoor Room

A RADIANT FLOOR HEATING SYSTEM can be used outdoors to warm up porches, porticos, and even pool decks. The system utilizes a series of water-filled cables laid on top of subflooring, covered with a thin layer of concrete or other substrate, and then topped with flooring materials such as wood, tile, flagstone, or decorative concrete. Unlike traditional heating systems, which warm the air, a radiant floor heating system concentrates heat in the floor, where it radiates warmth safely and efficiently to bare feet. Even the furniture will be warmed by heat coming up from the floor.

A Dream Deck

SOME HOMES HAVE DRAMATIC OCEAN OR MOUNTAIN VISTAS, but most homeowners are content with views of backyard gardens, small groves of trees, or emerald patches of lawn. Overlooking backyard views and open to the sky, a deck offers a sense of freedom and expansiveness from a protected position near the house. Although a deck is usually attached to one or more walls of a house, it provides a greater sense of connection to the landscape because it is uncovered. It can be located off one or more rooms, wrap around a house, or cascade down a hillside in a series of multilevel platforms that can create varied areas for relaxing, gathering, cooking, or dining.

▶ DECKS PERCHED HIGH above the yard serve as promontories—offering expansive views while maintaining a comfortable connection with the house. The sloping hillside and partial enclosure (on three sides) of these decks accentuate their role as promontories.

◄ COPPER PICKETS and a pineapple finial dress up this redwood deck. Lattice screens the neighbor's house from view, while a beam trellis provides a strong support for vines. Together, these elements frame a view of an old oak tree.

▼ THIS LOW DECK is located just beyond the kitchen, making it a convenient spot for meals. It is built just above ground level, eliminating the need for railings. A perennial border provides a buffer between the deck and steep hillside that leads to the lake below.

▶ THE ROUND TABLE, box planter, chair backs, and railing echo the curve of this deck. The deck extends out from the house, much like a dock into a harbor, to bring the dining area closer to the water's edge.

◀ A DECK WITHOUT RAILINGS offers unobstructed views to the surrounding landscape. In some municipalities, a deck without railings is permitted as long as it isn't more than 36 in. off the ground. In other municipalities, railings may be required for decks that are 18 in., 20 in., or 30 in. off the ground. Be sure to check local codes before designing and building a deck.

Materials Planning Pays Off

BEFORE DESIGNING A DECK, it's smart to check the available sizes, bulk quantities, and pricing of wood planks used for flooring. Because wood availability and pricing fluctuates, you may want to look at several board sizes. Most wood planks are sold as 8-ft., 10-ft., 12-ft., or 16-ft. boards, and 12-ft. boards are often the least expensive to buy per running foot. Overall deck lengths in multiples of 8 ft., 10 ft., or 12 ft. will result in the least amount of waste; a 12-ft., 24-ft., or 36-ft.-long deck that uses 12-ft. boards could be the most cost efficient to build.

▼THIS DECK HELPS unite the house with the surrounding landscape by extending far into the yard and gently cascading down the gradual slope. Rough-hewn benches, which double as low deck railings, give the deck a natural, woodsy look.

▲A DISTINCTIVE RAILING—which includes the posts and pickets, as well as caps and finials—can give a deck personality. These "twig" railings and oversized wooden posts visually connect the deck with the home's rustic architecture, while framing the view of the lake.

SEATING CAN BE positioned many ways on a deck. Here, chairs face out to the view. They could also be clustered in several conversation groups or pulled up around a table. A single chair off by itself provides a contemplative space.

IF THE VIEW from a deck is to a lower area, such as this garden, consider railings that enhance the view. Wrought iron replaces the usual wooden pickets in this railing, creating a sturdy structure without restricting the view.

◄ THIS BROAD, TIERED DECK features both upper and lower gathering spaces—one for dining and the other for sunbathing. The two spaces are connected to each other and the house by a transitional landing and stairs. Built-in planter boxes and custom railings give the spaces color and character and help tie all the elements together.

A DISTINCTIVE DECK DRAIN

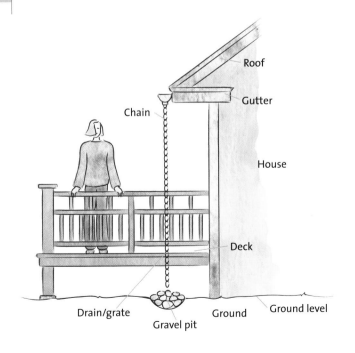

Roof

Gutter

Chain

House

Deck

Drain/grate

Gravel pit

Ground

Ground level

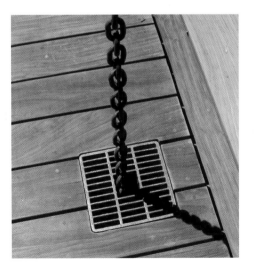

▲ INSTEAD OF A TRADITIONAL DOWNSPOUT, a large chain hanging from the eaves is used to direct the water from the gutter to the ground. An iron drain cover allows the water to pass through the deck's surface. Spacing between planks prevents water from accumulating on the deck.

▲ AN ABUNDANCE OF PLANTINGS makes this tiered deck feel like it's an integral part of the garden. Flower beds come up to the edge, container plantings are scattered about the deck, and vines are working their way across an arbor. The upper level even extends out over a water garden.

▶ THIS HOME FEATURES two small decks: a private space off the upstairs bedroom and a lower deck off the main floor for entertaining and dining. Laying boards on a diagonal alters the perspective on the lower deck, making it look larger than it is.

DECKS THAT EXTEND from upper floors offer bird's-eye views of back-yard landscapes. This deck features cut-stone flooring that matches the pool edging below. The sturdy railings complement the architecture of the house.

Room to Dine Comfortably

THERE ARE SOME GUIDELINES ON HOW MANY **people** an outdoor table will accommodate and how it will fit into your backyard space. A 26-in. round bistro table will seat two, a 48-in. round or square table will seat four to six, and a 36-in. by 72-in. rectangular table will seat up to eight. Side chairs average 17 in. wide and deep, while armchairs run closer to 24 in. wide and deep.

Although tables tend to stay put, chairs are often pushed in and out, and even shuffled about a space. A good rule of thumb for a cozy yet comfortable space is the width or length of the table plus at least 3 ft. on each side. That provides ample room for getting in and out of chairs and space for someone to slide by for serving or clearing dishes. For a more open feeling or greater flexibility in the arrangement of furniture, allow extra room. If there are steps nearby, be sure to leave at least 5 ft. between the table and steps for safety.

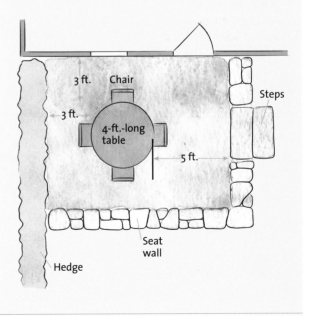

3 ft.   Chair

Steps

3 ft.

4-ft.-long table

5 ft.

Seat wall

Hedge

▶ DECKS AND PATIOS surround this house. A small upper deck provides a quiet place to sit outside the living room. A large mid-level deck features an outdoor kitchen and space for entertaining. A lower patio provides a casual place for relaxing near the family room.

▼ A DECK DOESN'T HAVE TO BE attached to a house. This low, freestanding deck offers a destination in the landscape. Regardless of where a deck is built, the flooring should be raised at least 6 in. off the ground to provide adequate ventilation and help prevent rot.

◄ BUILT-IN SEATING can be installed along the outside edge of a deck or placed against the house, as shown here. Built-in benches provide casual seating and can help accommodate a crowd when entertaining.

▼ DECKS SUIT HOUSES on steep hillsides. This one has a deck that wraps around the house, extends toward the edge of the property, and then cascades down steps to a stone patio and small lawn. The configuration makes the yard more accessible and inviting.

◄ STAINLESS-STEEL CABLE PORCH RAILINGS complement the contemporary architecture of this beach house. The cable is noncorrosive and may be attached to wood, carbon-steel pipe, structural tubing, or stainless-steel posts.

A Patio and Terrace Link to the Landscape

A PATIO OR TERRACE is a paved outdoor area that frequently links the indoors and out. Although the terms are used interchangeably, terrace refers more specifically to a "shelf" on a sloping site. The flooring may echo a home's interior materials, as in the case of matching tile, brick, or decorative concrete, or it may more closely relate to the natural environment, as with stone or pea gravel. Walls formed by the house, freestanding masonry walls, fences, hedges, or mixed plantings help create a greater sense of privacy and coziness around a patio or terrace. Its roof may be an arbor, a canopy of trees, or left open to the sky. A patio or terrace can be made more livable with a fireplace, outdoor kitchen, comfortable seating, and outdoor lighting. Plants placed along the edge of a patio or terrace connect the space to the surrounding landscape.

▼ THIS TERRACE is built close to the ground, but the low wall provides a sense of enclosure and offers additional seating. The wall is constructed with a fieldstone base and flagstone cap; the terrace is built from oversized slabs of the same fieldstone.

◄ THIS SMALL FLAGSTONE PATIO is enclosed on all sides—either by the house, stone walls, or a water feature—to create an intimate space for an alfresco dinner. Colorful lanterns hang from a rustic arbor, adding a decorative touch and illuminating the space after dark.

▲ THE DESIGN AND MATERIALS of this small stone patio unite the home and the landscape. The patio flows from the back door and across the stream into the yard. The stones in the patio, pillars, steps, and water feature all match in color for a uniform appearance, although they vary in shape, size, and cut.

Creating Inviting Side Yard Transitions

THE SIDE YARD IS ONE OF THE MOST NEGLECTED SPACES in a residential landscape. When it's tucked between two houses, the sliver of yard can be dark and narrow. On a larger lot, it is often little more than an unused expanse of lawn or woods.

Most often, a side yard is a passageway that connects the front yard and backyard—although, if backyard space is limited, it might double as an outdoor room. Because a side yard is exposed to the street and neighboring house, the key to making it inviting is to create privacy. Erecting a fence or wall on a narrow lot will do the job. Adding a pergola overhead will enhance the sense of passage and screen views from the neighbor's upstairs rooms. In a spacious side yard, hedges, trees, or mixed plantings of perennials, grasses, shrubs, and trees along the periphery will provide desired screening.

An arbor or gate placed near the front of the house makes the path through the side yard more inviting. Plantings give the passageway more visual texture. Adding a focal point—such as a sculpture or water feature—at the far end of the side yard's path will draw you into the space.

▲ THIS GRAY-STAINED PERGOLA creates an inviting passageway through a narrow side yard while increasing privacy for the homeowners. Without the evergreen-vine-draped crosspieces, neighbors in their upstairs bedrooms could see into the downstairs rooms of this house.

▶ THIS SMALL, INFORMAL PATIO of dry-laid, rounded cobblestone was designed for the homeowners' enjoyment. A larger patio with smoother flooring and additional seating would be more suitable for entertaining.

▼ MOST PATIOS are built adjacent to a house. This one was built a short stroll away—against a retaining wall along the edge of the lawn where it can be viewed from indoors. It is accompanied by a bench and fishpond.

▲BRICK FLOORS are perfect for small spaces, where they can be laid in myriad patterns without looking busy. When covering large expanses of ground, brick tends to look busy unless other paving materials with broader surfaces—such as stone or concrete—are mixed into the design.

◄ RAISED SEATING AREAS are more comfortable when they are protected and private. The stone retaining wall and side walls that wrap around the table and bench make this small patio feel even more intimate.

▼ A TERRACE WITH a random shape and irregular edges, like this one, is less formal than a geometrically designed space. Here, mounded plantings and large boulders create a gradual transition into the land-scape, making the patio feel as if it naturally grew out of the space.

▼PLACE FURNITURE FAR ENOUGH away from doors so that the traffic flow remains uninterrupted, even on small patios like this one. Chairs clustered in corners also feel cozier than similar groupings in the middle of a patio.

▲AN L- OR U-SHAPED HOUSE creates lots of opportunities for patios. This patio connects interior rooms and serves as a pass-through, increasing overall traffic and activity in the space. The homeowners gain additional privacy and protection from windy weather because the walls of the house partially screen the patio.

▲A SUNKEN PATIO like the one just beyond this basement door is cozy and private. The surrounding stacked-stone retaining walls and juniper groundcovers prevent soil erosion on the sloped site. The walls also add texture and a feeling of warmth to the seating area.

►A WALL OF PLANTS provides privacy around this brick patio, making it a comfortable space for a casual family dinner. Colorful tropical plants such as bananas, gingers, hibiscus, and coleus mingle among trees and shrubs to obscure views and establish boundaries.

Expressive Materials Make a Difference

SPECIAL MATERIALS used in small doses can upgrade your backyard into a one-of-a-kind oasis. For example, a tiny gathering space can be made into a unique spot when you focus on the details. It's a place to splurge on distinctive paving materials, favorite plants, or the perfect chair.

Mixing and matching materials is another effective way to add expressive materials to the landscape. Build a picket fence atop a low stone wall, or combine stone and brick in a path. Seek out materials with unique qualities, such as textured tile or colorful river cobbles, or combine materials with contrasting textures and colors such as red brick and bluestone pavers.

▼THIS PORCH AND PATIO occupy neighboring spaces with similar views yet are very different places. One is sheltered against the house and under a roof; the other is spacious and exposed to the elements. They are separated by boulders, grassy plantings, and a change in elevation.

▲BUCKETS OF PEBBLES and a few bags of concrete mix are the tools landscape designer Jeffrey Bale uses to turn a patio floor into a work of art. Patience, creativity, and elbow grease are all that's needed to create inexpensive pebble-and-tile mosaics like this one.

▲ON THIS HILLSIDE, terracing is used to connect a series of outdoor rooms. The transition between the two patios is marked by an opening in a trellised wall, a narrowing of the steps, and step materials that differ from the paving surfaces.

▲ CLUSTERED POTS help define a dining area on this raised patio. The
white spikes of gayfeather in the foreground and distance mark corners
of this outdoor room, while foliage plants offer long-season good looks.

▲ THE SOOTHING SOUND of water encourages relaxation. The trickling fountain in this backyard serves as a focal point and creates an inviting getaway. The edging around the pool provides a place for the owners' daughter to watch and feed the fish.

▶ CITY DWELLERS often transform rooftops into terraces filled with container plantings. Rooftops can be ideal spots to grow herbs and vegetables, perfect accompaniments to alfresco dining. Shrubs and small trees are also appropriate container plantings, as long as they are secured to withstand windy days.

Planting Pockets Soften Paving

THE HARD SURFACES AND EDGES of stone or brick patio floors look softer with the addition of plantings. Greenery that sprawls as it grows will naturally conceal corners and edges of hard flooring. There's another planting method that gives a patio an even more custom look: Remove some brick, stone, or tile pavers in a defined or random pattern in and about the patio. Doing this will expose soil-filled pockets for plantings.

Though planting pockets can be as narrow as the ½-in. crack between two pavers, most plants will appreciate an amended planting pocket that is at least 1 ft. wide. Compact shrubs and trees can be tucked into pockets that are 2 ft. to 3 ft. wide.

▼THIS ARBOR-COVERED TERRACE has a captivating water feature that runs its length. A recirculating runnel, or channel of water, flows across the terrace, tumbles down the steps, and spills into a fishpond below.

▶THIS CURVED TERRACE protrudes into the yard and adjoins a portico and raised patio. The terrace serves both as a transition to the lawn and as a gathering space for dining and entertaining. Terracotta tile, which is only durable in moderate climates, visually connects the three spaces.

▲EVEN ON A GENTLE SLOPE, a patio can ease the grade change from the house to the lawn. The patio shown here is located just beyond the kitchen, where it serves as a convenient spot for parents to watch their young children play nearby.

◄TALL, SCULPTURAL PILLARS create a grand entrance to this raised patio. Raising a patio slightly above the surrounding grade calls special attention to the seating area.

Showcasing Outdoor Art

A COURTYARD OR PATIO is an intimate space in which to showcase outdoor art. A single piece of art will make a stronger statement than multiple pieces that compete for attention, although collections can be showcased effectively by limiting the number of pieces that are seen from any given location. Some sculptural pieces are meant to stand alone as the focal point on a patch of lawn or in the center of a courtyard. Other pieces of art stand out with a backdrop of plantings.

The type of plantings you use to highlight a piece of art will be determined by the object's material and shape. Plants with intricate foliage create a sharp contrast with bold, smooth surfaces. Ornamental grasses envelop architectural artifacts or sculpture with well-defined edges in a soft setting. Mounding plants hide the base of sculptures, allowing the eye to focus on the art's expressive qualities.

Choose a meaningful spot for outdoor art. Place a contemporary sculpture, mobile, found object, architectural artifact, or more traditional cast-stone statuary where it serves as a focal point along a wall, at the end of a path, in a border, or at the center of a formal garden. For maximum benefit, place an object where it is visible from an indoor room as well.

▲ SOFT PLANTINGS on this patio complement the carved-stone faces and granite-ball fountain. The sculptures are located just beyond the back door, where they can be enjoyed from both indoors and out.

◄ THE KEY TO COMBINING STONES is to strike a balance between contrast and uniformity. The smooth-surfaced, cut-granite pavers on this patio differ in texture and style from the random stone used in the walls, yet they are similar in color. Both look at home in this New England landscape.

▼THIS SMALL PATIO is laid in several brick patterns and utilizes odd-sized remainders—an approach reminiscent of the brickbat paving used in Colonial Williamsburg or the clinker brick paving from the Arts and Crafts era. This carefree style suits the rustic charm of the cottage.

▲PATIOS CAN BE DESTINATIONS placed away from the house. This patio, just large enough for a table and chairs, is tucked into a hillside next to a recirculating waterfall and pond, offering a relaxing escape with a view of the house.

▼CREEPING THYME, Corsican mint, small sedums, and blue star creeper thrive even when tucked between the dry-laid, random flagstone pavers on this sunken patio. They can all handle light foot traffic, and the thyme and mint release a sweet fragrance when stepped upon.

▲THE PATIO IS SEAMLESSLY built into the curving path that winds through this Florida backyard. The brick edging creates a sense of fluidity and motion in a small space, and the canopy of trees provides shady relief on warm days.

Outdoor Rooms on a Budget

AN INVITING GATHERING SPACE doesn't have to break the bank. Start small and expand or upgrade as funds allow. Here are a few ideas for keeping costs down:

- Place outdoor rooms near the house to take advantage of shared conveniences such as kitchens, baths, lighting, and stereo systems.
- If supplemental lighting is required, look into easy-to-install solar lighting kits, utilize oil lanterns, or bring out the candles.
- Cook over a freestanding charcoal or gas grill, or build your own fire pit.
- Create walls from plants or stock fencing materials. Quick-growing vines will cover inexpensive fencing materials.
- Go eclectic—gather rustic furnishings from flea markets and antique malls. A fresh coat of paint will do wonders for worn furniture.
- Convert an antique tub, ceramic pot, or wood trough into a water feature.
- Warm up your surroundings with a portable fire pit or chiminea.
- Keep construction simple. It's easy to spread crushed gravel yourself, for example. Accent gravel floors with sections of irregular flagstone or cobblestone edging.

▲A TWIG OR BAMBOO FENCE covered with fast-growing vines makes quick and inexpensive screening. This type of structure will last several years. At that time, it can either be rebuilt, or a more permanent fence can be constructed.

▶ THIS PATIO IS PAVED with bricks that radiate out from a central point in a circular pattern, ringed by a boxwood hedge, and accented with a round dining table. The repetition of circular elements creates a sense of unity and formality in the landscape.

▲ FLAGSTONE CAN BE LAID in multiple ways in the same yard. It is mortared and edged in brick on the patio and adjacent path. On connecting paths, it is dry-laid with a random edge. In the garden, it is used for steps along a gravel path.

▶ THIS ASYMMETRICAL PATIO calls attention to itself because of the random pattern of its stone flooring. The pattern and light color of the stone provide a dramatic contrast to the surrounding plantings.

▶ THIS BROAD, STONE PATIO breaks up an expanse of lawn. Positioned in an open area, the space is suitable for a party, outdoor wedding, or other social event. The retaining wall handles overflow seating.

▶ NOT ALL PATIOS are spacious enough for large gatherings or even for lingering very long. The white café table and chairs anchoring this petite patio simply offer a spot to pause while exploring the garden.

Getting Creative with Concrete

ONSIDER CONCRETE for the look of stone, brick, or tile without the cost. Stamped and stained, concrete bears a remarkable resemblance to other masonry materials. Although concrete still comes in the ubiquitous gray, it is also available in an array of colors, textures, and finishes. It can be mixed with aggregate, tinted with stain, brushed with sand, or stamped into patterns. It can be precast, polished, and laid like cut stone. Concrete can also be formed into interlocking block pavers and arranged into patterns. In cold climates where concrete is less commonly used, special reinforcements added to the concrete help eliminate heaving during the winter.

▼THIS SMALL PATIO, which is tucked into a hillside, is paved in dry-laid, cut-granite cobblestones and hugged by evergreen shrubs and ground covers to create a calm, cozy space.

▲THIS PATIO is designed as a series of broad steps on a gentle slope. What makes this design so successful is the mix of paving materials with contrasting textures, the addition of a water feature, and the selective use of upright pergolas.

PATIOS AND PLANTING BEDS are good alternatives to lawn—especially in small backyards where space is at a premium. Eliminating the lawn reduces routine maintenance chores, and mixed plantings with small ornamental trees, shrubs, and perennials keep the backyard interesting throughout the seasons.

CONTAINER PLANTS can be easily used to spruce up a patio and give color to large expanses of wall space. The large pots on the patio just beyond the back door of this New Orleans home hold citrus trees, bamboo, and a water garden with papyrus.

WATER FEATURES

▶ THIS RUNNEL draws visitors from the upper deck to the lower garden as they follow the water across the patio and down the steps. The water is then transported back up to the small fountain on the deck, where it begins its journey again.

▼ GRADE CHANGES in a landscape offer excellent opportunities for creating water features with cascades or waterfalls. This 3-ft. cascade is enhanced by the contrast in shape and size of the large, rough-tumbled, rectangular stones and the smaller, round, river-washed stones.

▼THIS SMALL FISHPOND is edged with stones and filled with water lilies, water lettuce, and papyrus. It includes a softly gurgling urn fountain. Both the moving water and fish help keep mosquitoes at bay, yet birds still find the pond attractive.

▼ALTHOUGH THE WATER is recirculated from the pond by a pump, this small water feature looks and sounds like a spring because water trickles out from beneath the stones. The rough, mossy stones enhance the natural-looking setting.

◄WALL FOUNTAINS come in all shapes, sizes, and styles and can be built into freestanding or retaining walls. The sound of the water splashing into the pool below is determined by the volume of water trickling out of the fountain, the distance the water falls, and the depth of the pool.

OUTDOOR FURNITURE

◄ OUTDOOR TABLES come in nearly as many shapes and sizes as indoor tables, seating from 2 to 12 people. Some have hideaway leaves to adjust the length. Others fold up easily so they can be stored for winter.

▼ TEAK IS A POPULAR MATERIAL for patio and garden furniture because it gracefully weathers to a soft gray color, resists splintering, and comes in a range of traditional and contemporary styles.

▲ THE SAME CARE SHOULD BE GIVEN to choosing outdoor chairs as given to selecting interior furniture, and comfort is a top priority. Select from among cushioned armchairs, side chairs, sofas, chairs with ottomans, and lounges, as well as garden benches, gliders, rockers, and porch swings.

New Furniture Choices

FURNITURE MANUFACTURERS **have responded to our increased passion for decorating outdoor rooms with stylish furniture made from a variety of materials.** In addition to teak, red cedar, molded plastic, and wrought iron—which have long been outdoor favorites—choices for outdoor furniture now include cast aluminum, galvanized metal dipped in a zinc bath, rust-resistant steel with an enamel finish, faux wicker, and exotic woods. All furnishings can be made more comfortable with the addition of fast-drying, water- and mildew-resistant cushions, which come in an infinite range of colors and styles.

▲ PATIO FURNITURE is formed from many different materials. Metal chairs, such as these, are among the strongest, most durable options and include steel, cast iron, wrought iron, and galvanized aluminum. Each of these metals can be painted, zinc-dipped, or treated with a polyester top coat to prevent rust.

▶ WATER- AND MILDEW-RESISTANT cushions add style and comfort to outdoor furnishings. Cushion fabrics come in a wide range of colors and patterns and can be coordinated with indoor décor, an outdoor decorating theme, or plants and garden accessories.

BUILT-IN SEATING

▶ ALTHOUGH THIS RUSTIC STONE BENCH IS CONSTRUCTED more for visual interest than for comfort, it is quite functional. It helps retain a steep bank, while providing a casual place to pause for a special view or to set tools when working in the garden.

▼ A BUILT-IN BENCH can be a practical alternative to a deck railing. It increases seating in a small space to help accommodate a crowd. With some ingenuity and a few hinges for doors, the space beneath the seats can convert into outdoor storage space.

▼THIS CURVED STONE SEATING is built to last. Cushions soften the stone, and slabs built higher than the seating are used as end tables. The bench, with its backdrop of exotic greenery, is the focal point of this backyard patio.

Building a Wall at Sitting Height

ALOW WALL SERVES MANY ROLES. It can define the edge of a patio or terrace, create a sense of enclosure without making a space feel "closed in," and provide extra seating without taking up additional space. To make the wall comfortable for sitting, build it 14 in. to 16 in. high and at least 12 in. wide. For masonry walls, make sure the cap (top piece) is a smooth surface that won't snag clothing. A cap in a contrasting material from the wall, such as bluestone on brick or stucco, will add a distinct look to a backyard.

▼ A WALL AROUND A PATIO can double as seating as long as it has a reasonably smooth surface and is built at a comfortable sitting height. The board that sits atop this masonry retaining wall carves out a spot for a quiet break next to a garden stream.

▲ THE HEAVY WOODEN BENCH built into a nook along this retaining
wall also serves as the base of a pergola. The structure is draped in
vines, creating a cool place to enjoy the surrounding garden.

A Peaceful Courtyard

THE CONFIGURATION OF A COURTYARD makes it an inherently quiet, secluded place. Though it may be open to the sky, a courtyard is enclosed on three or more sides, creating a gathering space that is protected by the house and surrounding walls. In some cases, it may even serve as a passageway between rooms of the house.

When designing a courtyard, it's important to include a shady spot for the seating—perhaps beneath a tree, umbrella, or an eyebrow arbor attached to the house. By providing a glimpse of the views beyond the courtyard through a gate, window, or gap in the courtyard wall, the area will feel more spacious. And finally, the addition of vines, planting pockets, or raised or container plantings will soften the look of hard surfaces around the courtyard.

▲ MANY TREES WILL ADAPT to the confines of a courtyard and, once established, provide an overhead canopy of shade and shelter. Trees commonly grown along sidewalks—such as star magnolias, redbuds, and pollarded sycamores—are good choices for courtyards.

◄ THIS NEW ORLEANS-STYLE HOME features French doors and full-length glass windows that open onto a courtyard. The large expanse of glass makes the interior rooms brighter and the courtyard seem larger than it would if surrounded by solid walls.

▼THE WINDOWLIKE OPENING in this brightly colored gate helps open up an otherwise enclosed backyard space, expanding views and improving cross-ventilation. Similar openings can also be built into masonry walls, framed in fences, and cut out of dense hedges.

◄DETAILS CAN MAKE A BIG difference in a small space. The stone pattern in this small courtyard might look busy if it were used in a large space. Here, it has the same effect as a throw rug or runner used to accent a room.

▲BRIGHT COLORS suit courtyards—especially those surrounded by tall walls or buildings that tend to make the spaces shady. Not only will bright colors feel more cheerful, they will also reflect more natural light around the courtyard than dark colors, which simply absorb light.

►CLINGING VINES, such as climbing hydrangea or Boston ivy, will soften a brick or concrete wall. Climbing roses, twining vines, and vines with tendrils need additional support and occasional guidance, which can be provided by a trellis mounted an inch or two from the wall.

Designing a Wall or Fence

WALLS AND FENCES **serve many roles in the landscape. They separate spaces, create privacy, add a vertical accent where needed, and provide a backdrop for colorful plantings. They can also frame special views, screen unwanted ones, and help buffer neighborhood noise.**

Walls are built as low as 1 ft. high, while fences can be built as high as 8 ft. They may be made from wood, brick, stone, interlocking blocks, or stucco. Their height and design are meant to send a clear message. For example, a low, painted fence with widely spaced pickets encour- ages friendly conversation. A tall, solid masonry wall indicates a desire for privacy.

Openings, such as windows and doorways, can enhance a fence or wall. Arbors, arches, and posts can frame a doorway, offering a glimpse beyond, while a gate adds character to a wall or fence.

To give a wall color and texture, think about what kind of material will give you the intended result. A stacked-stone wall has a rough surface and natural finish. A brick, block, or stucco wall has a course texture and comes in a variety of colors. Wood fences may have smooth or rough surfaces and can be painted or stained in any imaginable color.

▲ THIS COURTYARD, which is anchored by a tall, masonry retaining wall, was designed to create an inviting backyard space on a large, sloping lot. It includes a pea-gravel sitting area, a small lawn, fountain, and 3-ft.-deep flower borders.

▲ IN SMALL COURTYARDS surrounded by tall walls, plants will help reduce the noise that bounces off hard surfaces. Grow vines on walls, build raised flower beds, create planting pockets, or add containers and window boxes filled with favorite plants to soften sounds.

Cooking Out

THE OUTDOOR KITCHEN IS THE ULTIMATE LUXURY AND CONVENIENCE in outdoor living. Not only does it keep the heat out of the house in summertime, but having an outdoor cooking area also reduces the number of trips made to the indoor kitchen. As a result, more time can be spent enjoying the outdoors.

The grill is at the heart of an outdoor kitchen. Freestanding grills are popular, affordable, and available in a wide range of styles. A fully equipped outdoor kitchen, however, can transform the backyard barbecue into a gourmet gathering. Today's grills feature optional smoker boxes, side burners, rotisseries, woks, warming racks, and more. Weatherproof kitchen cabinets serve as host to bar sinks, beer taps, compact refrigerators, and storage drawers. Outdoor outlets offer a convenient place to plug in lights, radios, and blenders. Durable, all-weather countertops make serving a convenience and may be designed as counter seating with pull-up stools.

▼ TO KEEP SMOKE OUT of guests' eyes, place a grill away from seating areas and on the downwind side of a patio and deck. This grill is positioned along one side of a deck and under an open-roofed structure to help define and enclose the space.

A GENEROUS LENGTH of counter space flanks this oversized grill to make serving a crowd easy. It is built against a wall of the house under several sconces used to illuminate the counter space and grill at night.

THIS BARBECUE COUNTER has wood siding and is painted to match the house. The 13-ft.-long counter includes a 30-in.-long grill, dual side burners, an under-counter refrigerator, a stainless-steel sink, storage drawers, and an electrical outlet. The doors beneath the sink and grill give homeowners access to appliances and storage.

Choosing the Right Grill

IF YOU HAVEN'T SHOPPED FOR A GRILL IN A WHILE, **you're in for a surprise. Before heading for the hearth and patio store, home center, or hardware store, beef up your knowledge of grill features:**

- **Portability:** Some units are easy to move; others are heavy, permanently connected to gas lines, or built into counters.
- **Fuel:** Charcoal grills give food a smoky flavor, but it takes time to build a hot fire. Gas grills are easy to light and offer greater control over temperature. Charcoal grills with gas starters offer the best of both. Electric grills are environmentally friendly and easy to clean. And infrared grills radiate heat at very high temperatures, which makes searing meats a snap.
- **BTU:** British Thermal Units are a measure of heat energy. Most average-sized grills with two burners should have 30,000 to 50,000 BTU. If you live in a cold region of the country, a grill with higher BTU may work more efficiently. (In moderate climates, you'll just use more fuel with a higher BTU grill.)
- **Accessories:** Accessory choices include side burners, smoker boxes, warming racks, rotisseries, woks, lights, carts, cabinetry, and more.
- **Pricing:** Prices range from less than $100 for a small portable grill to as much as $10,000 for a top-of-the-line grill with all the bells and whistles.

◄ PROFESSIONAL-QUALITY, freestanding grills offer more grilling space and options than small, portable grills but are more affordable and occupy less space than custom-built outdoor kitchens. This 36-in. stainless-steel grill has a 12-in. dual side burner for simmering sauces, steaming vegetables, and cooking rice.

A TRADITIONAL WOOD-BURNING OVEN—which has its roots in Italy—has been custom designed and built for this pizza lover and outdoor chef. The oven reaches temperatures exceeding 400 degrees and can also be used for baking breads, roasting vegetables, and cooking meat dishes.

▲ THIS ADOBE-STYLE PATIO features a raised fire pit—topped with river cobbles for a decorative accent—used to warm up the space. Like most fire pits, it can be fitted with a grill for cooking. Dry-wood storage is conveniently located nearby.

◄ BARBECUE GRILL UNITS can be dropped in or slid into stone walls. This drop-in unit is built into a mortared, fieldstone retaining wall. It includes a side burner, warming rack, and a countertop made from bluestone. A slide-in unit would feature stainless-steel storage beneath the grill.

▶THIS PAVILION has plenty of space to entertain with room for a grill, ancillary outdoor appliances, counter space, and storage. The bar arrangement enables the chef to converse with guests while preparing a meal.

▼THESE HORNOS, or adobe bread ovens, are modeled after those used by Native Americans throughout the Southwest. Today, hornos are built from sun-dried, mud bricks that are either handmade or purchased at an adobe brickyard, and then bonded together with mud mortar.

◀THIS OUTDOOR KITCHEN features a drop-in gas grill and bar sink, plus several storage drawers and cabinets built into the brick wall. It is located beneath the shelter of a portico, where it is protected from the rain but exposed enough to let the smoke escape from the dining space.

▲A GRILL located on an interior wall of a pavilion needs a hood to vent smoke away from the enclosed space. This grill has a copper hood and matching wall sconces that will acquire a verdigris patina as they age.

◄THIS CHARCOAL GRILL is built at the end of a swimming-pool deck and has flanking brick-and-bluestone walls for additional seating. The adjustable rack inside the grill can be dropped for small fires during family dinners and raised for large fires when hosting poolside parties.

▶ THIS WRAPAROUND KITCHEN surrounds the chef with counter space, making it easy to serve drinks and meals to many guests at once. The umbrella provides shelter for guests and food. The gas lamp illuminates the cooking and eating areas after dark.

▲ THIS L-SHAPED COUNTER creates convenient grilling and serving areas that accommodate counter-style or buffet-style dining. L-shaped counters are the outdoor equivalent of the efficient "work triangle" often used to design indoor kitchens.

▶ LIGHTING IS AN IMPORTANT ASPECT of outdoor kitchen design. Chefs need to see when the food is finished cooking, and guests like to see what they are being served. The owners of this grill mounted a small spotlight on the fence to shine directly onto the cooking surface.

Building an Outdoor Kitchen

WHEN PLANNING AN OUTDOOR KITCHEN, consider how accessible it will be to water, gas, and electricity. An outdoor kitchen placed against one wall of a house makes it easier to tap into utilities. As an added benefit, a roof overhang will help shelter outdoor appliances.

You'll probably want to hire a professional to do this kind of work, but here are a few things to consider. A kitchen built in a location far away from the house will involve digging trenches for supply lines. Check with your municipality regarding building codes for the required distance between gas and power lines. Be sure to ask if you need one or two separate trenches to accommodate the lines.

For a bar sink, refrigerator, and icemaker, plan on adding a cold-water line. Hot-water lines are rarely needed outdoors unless you plan to add a dishwasher. Remember to install adequate waste-water drainage for sinks and refrigerators.

◄ YOU CAN CREATE outdoor kitchens using a wide range of appliances. This kitchen includes a five-burner gas grill, double and single side burners, storage drawers, and a refrigerator. Other common amenities include bar sinks and warming drawers.

Keeping Warm

WHAT BETTER WAY IS THERE TO CREATE AMBIENCE than with the warm glow of an outdoor hearth? A fireplace knocks off the chill in northern or high-altitude regions where summer evenings are cool and in warmer climates where outdoor living is enjoyed well into the winter. A fire pit, fire dish, luminaria, or chiminea will warm up a small area of the outdoors. For a bolder aesthetic statement or more warmth, install a manufactured or custom-built fireplace of brick, stone, tile, or stucco, and accent it with an attractive mantel. Another option for warming an outdoor area is a patio heater, which comes in floor, tabletop, and wall-mounted models. Safe fuel options for outdoor hearths run the gamut from wood and manufactured logs to propane, natural gas, and proprietary gels, which vary in cost and portability.

◄ A STACKED-STONE CHIMNEY looks at home on the exterior wall of this traditional house. The outdoor fireplace is a welcome surprise. A single chimney can support an indoor and an outdoor fireplace as long as separate flues are used for safety and drawing efficiency.

◄ THIS OUTDOOR-ROOM arrangement offers the best of both worlds—the shelter and warmth of a partially enclosed structure with a built-in fireplace, and the bright, open space of an adjoining patio. The tile flooring ties both areas together.

▲ AN OUTDOOR FIREPLACE with gas-burning logs helps relieve the chill of frosty mornings and nippy evenings beneath this backyard pavilion. Today's gas logs produce yellow flames that resemble those created by real wood.

◄ WHEN PLANNING FOR AN OUTDOOR FIREPLACE, keep in mind the space needed for firewood. In addition to easily accessible stacks of dry, seasoned wood, it is convenient to have a small, sheltered bin for wood within an arm's reach of the fire.

FIRE PITS are traditionally placed in the center of an outdoor area to create inviting social spaces for larger groups. Several sides of this fire pit are surrounded with seating to accommodate many guests.

A FIREPLACE creates a special ambiance in an outdoor room. The yellow flames of a fire add visual—and physical—warmth to this covered space, while recessed ceiling fixtures provide overhead light.

THE LARGER SCALE of an outdoor space differs from an indoor room. That is why this heavy, oversized fireplace fits in so well against a hillside. A smaller fireplace would be a better choice underneath a pavilion and a portico.

▲ THIS MASONRY FIREPLACE is constructed beyond the footprint of the portico, leaving plenty of room under the roof for dining or gathering around the large wooden table. A chimney diverts smoke away from the seating area.

▲ DRY-WOOD STORAGE can be built alongside the fireplace or into a nearby structure, such as this stacked-stone retaining wall. A masonry structure for wood storage is best because it won't be damaged by termites or other pests that may be attracted to firewood.

Burning Wood Responsibly

BURNING WOOD GENERATES EMISSIONS that may contribute to air pollution. To reduce the impact on the environment, build small, hot fires with dry, well-seasoned hardwood. Seasoned hardwood (dried for six months or longer to reduce the moisture content) is easy to light and burns long and efficiently. Consider burning manufactured logs or use alternative heating options such as pellet stoves, fireplace inserts, and EPA-certified clean-burning fireplaces. Also, be sure to use a chimney to raise the point at which the smoke releases. This will keep gathering spaces and neighboring yards free from smoke.

▶ THIS WOOD-BURNING FIRE PIT—reminiscent of a campground fireplace—is surrounded by a small stone patio and a rustic stone bench. Plantings on one side of the patio help screen the fire from prevailing winds.

▼ THE MATERIALS used to build this freestanding fireplace and chimney match those of the patio flooring, surrounding stone walls, and pergola posts. The raised hearth offers a convenient place to sit and warm up by the fire.

▶ THIS HEARTH AND SEAT WALL are built with the same stone and at the same height to keep the look uniform and to define the space without blocking views. The area beneath this raised hearth has a clever storage space for firewood.

▲PREFABRICATED OUTDOOR FIREPLACES—delivered by truck or trailer and easily installed—come in a wide range of styles, finishes, and sizes, making it easy to match the fireplace to your outdoor decor. This traditional brick version has gas-burning logs.

▼THIS PLAIN, CONCRETE-BLOCK outdoor fireplace was faced with flagstone to achieve the warmth and beauty of a traditional, more costly, and labor-intensive stacked-stone fireplace. The stone provides a striking yet natural contrast to the wooden deck.

▲A RAISED FIRE PIT can be constructed from stone, brick, tile, or stucco. This pit features a base of round cobbles capped with flagstone that match the stone used on the pergola posts, patio flooring, and outdoor kitchen.

Adding a Garden Structure

GARDEN STRUCTURES—whether arbors, pergolas, gazebos, or pavilions—make ideal settings for inviting outdoor rooms. Because most are designed as destinations, they serve as focal points in the landscape. Arbors and pergolas (extended arbors) are the simplest to construct because they have posts and an open framework overhead that beg to be draped in vines. The octagonal gazebo or larger, rectangular pavilion is also built with posts but has a solid roof overhead. Whether roofed or simply covered with vines, each structure offers a shady retreat for the backyard.

A structure as simple as a garden bench beneath an arbor or as elaborate as an outdoor kitchen, living room, and dining area incorporated into a generously sized pavilion creates a comfortable, inviting space. Sometimes, an arbor or a pergola is attached to a house—so it can provide shade for a patio, deck, or courtyard, as well as for the adjacent interior room. Although these structures are often made out of wood, they also come in other materials such as iron or copper or feature the addition of solid posts made out of brick, stacked stone, stucco, or concrete.

▲ A RAISED STRUCTURE built over a water feature has the feeling of a boardwalk or dock. This design brings the water closer to the sitting area. Also, by making this water seem to disappear beneath the structure, the stream appears to be larger than it is.

◄ A SIMPLE BENCH is transformed into a thronelike sitting area with the addition of a decorative arbor, brick flooring, and canopy of climbing roses. It protrudes slightly into the lawn, making it a place of importance in the landscape.

▲ THIS PAVILION is a commanding element in the landscape because it is positioned
at the end of a path. The fence that frames the path is painted in the same colors
as the pavilion.

▶ AN INTRICATELY DESIGNED ARBOR can be a reflection of special architectural details in a home. This Japanese-style arbor features openings with window boxes that have been planted in addition to curved details, which are echoed in the picnic table and benches.

▼ THIS PAVILION is built on a steep slope near a small waterfall and stream, creating an observation platform. It is constructed of redwood timbers with built-in seating and a copper roof.

◄ THIS PERGOLA is built on a patio near a back door and functions like a porch because it provides a sheltered space next to the house. It can be covered with vines to increase shade, soften the wooden surfaces, and add a splash of color.

▲ A RUSTIC STRUCTURE, like this gazebo, slips seamlessly into a woodland setting. The gazebo is constructed with rot-resistant black locust posts and rhododendron branch railings. The rhododendron branches will have a longer life span if they are treated with a sealer every other year.

◄ GARDEN STRUCTURES like this pergola should be designed with both the house and landscape in mind. In most cases, posts and beams should be similar in size to those on the house. However, oversized materials are called for against an expansive backdrop like this lake.

▲ THIS PERGOLA is the centerpiece of the backyard. It serves as a gathering place and marks the intersection of several paths that pass between the columns and lead to ornamental and kitchen gardens, a play area, and the house.

► LIGHT COLORS in a landscape always catch the eye first; that is why this painted white arbor stands out in contrast to the surrounding greenery. The arbor is a dominant element in the yard, so special attention was given to the design of the columns and ornate top.

◀ AN OPEN GARDEN STRUCTURE, such as this gazebo, feels cozier when it is placed against a solid backdrop of plantings. If an outdoor structure is located in too open a space, it may feel exposed. If it is set against other structures, it may look too busy.

Positioning a Gazebo

A GAZEBO IS A SUBSTANTIAL STRUCTURE **best suited to larger landscapes, and its positioning will affect how it is used. Placed close to the house or a pool, it will be used frequently for dining and gathering. Farther from the house, it serves as a getaway or destination for special occasions. Position a gazebo so it can be seen from indoors or from a special point in the yard—perhaps at the end of a winding path or as the only vertical element in a sweeping border. A gazebo placed high on a hillside will offer expansive views of the surrounding landscape.**

◀ THE WATER'S EDGE is always a favorite gathering space. By building seating along the sides of this pergola, it still functions as a passageway and frames a view of the pond. The structure is also large enough to accommodate a table and chairs to use on special occasions.

▲ BUILDING A PERGOLA against a tall stone, brick, or stucco retaining wall—especially one that forms a corner nook—creates a secluded and protected spot. The vines that are scrambling along the overhead beams enhance the pergola's sense of enclosure.

▶ ENCLOSING AN ARBOR on one side forms a comfortable and protected spot for a bench. This arbor, located along the edge of a lawn, becomes a focal point in the yard and a place from which to view activities.

▶ A GAZEBO is often placed along the periphery of a property where it becomes a destination and focal point. Tucked away in the backyard, this gazebo looks out over the curving borders of a woodland garden filled with tulips and daffodils in early spring.

▼ THIS ARBOR is tucked into a border of mixed plantings, where it becomes an integral part of the garden. Colorful container plantings enclose the open sides of the arbor, while bougainvillea scrambles up the sides and over the top.

Striking Vines for Arbors and Pergolas

WHEN CHOOSING A VINE, think beyond the flower colors. Select a vine with handsome foliage, fragrant flowers, or fall berries. Make sure the mature vine suits the size and stability of the structure. Here are a few praiseworthy vines for an arbor or pergola:

- American wisteria (*Wisteria frutescens* 'Amethyst Falls')
- Bougainvillea (*Bougainvillea spp.*)
- Carolina jessamine (*Gelsemium sempervirens*)
- Clematis (*Clematis spp.*)
- Climbing hydrangea (*Hydrangea petiolaris*)
- Climbing roses (*Rosa spp.*)
- Fiveleaf akebia (*Akebia quintata*)
- Golden hops (*Humulus lupulus* 'Aurea')
- Grape (*Vitis spp.*)
- Jasmine (*Jasminum polyanthum*)
- Porcelain berry (*Ampelopsis brevipedunculata*)
- Trumpet creeper (*Campsis radicans*)
- Virginia creeper (*Parthenocissus quinquefolia*)

▲SCREENING A GAZEBO can significantly increase its use and enjoyment while keeping out pesky insects. If electricity is available, adding a ceiling fan will keep the gnats away and cool things off on a muggy afternoon.

▲CLIMBING ROSES that stretch from 12 ft. to 30 ft. in length make ideal choices for arbors and pergolas. Since roses are not true climbers, but instead grasp onto supports with hooks (thorns), give them direction by loosely tying them to posts or trellises.

▶THE CONCRETE COLUMNS on this gazebo have a traditional appearance. Other materials such as wood, lightweight resin, metal, fiberglass, and cast stone are often used for arbor and pergola columns because they are durable and weather resistant. Overhead beams on most gazebos, such as this one, are built from pressure-treated or naturally rot-resistant lumber.

▼THIS CONTEMPORARY STRUCTURE, with a central gathering area, two passageways, and a peaked roof, was specifically designed to support a large, rambling rose. Roses are this gardener's preference, but wisteria, trumpet vine, and other large vines would also emphasize the unique shape of this structure.

Creating a Casual Seating Area

IT'S EASIER TO ESTABLISH CASUAL SEATING AREAS throughout the landscape than it is to plan a fully furnished outdoor room. Yet casual spaces can be just as inviting and are adaptable to any landscape and budget. All that's needed are a few comfortable chairs arranged on an open lawn, beneath the shade of an old tree, in a clearing in the woods, or on a knoll overlooking a favorite view. Create several seating areas—each with its own unique character—to enjoy at different times of day. For a quiet escape, set a garden bench in a small clearing surrounded by plants. For a comfortable place to watch the kids play, place a few lounge chairs along the edge of the lawn. To stimulate conversation, gather a circle of Adirondack chairs near a water feature. The more casual the seating area, the more inviting it will be.

▼ A PROMONTORY in the residential landscape is a prime outdoor seating area because it often overlooks a meadow, field, garden, pond, or hill. A sunrise or sunset is more compelling when viewed from a promontory.

▲ WHEN POSITIONED AT THE END of a path, a bench has draw-ing power. Not only does the path lead directly to it, but the bench also beckons to passersby to sit and relax. A small water feature makes this sitting area even more inviting.

◄ EVERYONE NEEDS a peaceful, secluded place to escape to from time to time. A quiet spot along a woodland path or adjacent to a pond or stream is the best spot for contem-plation and reflection. Even a simple bench, such as this stone slab, invites a pause for a meditative moment.

▲ A SIMPLE, OCTAGONAL tree bench is easy to build and lasts for years. The homeowners set their tools here while working in the garden and occasionally, when they have a chance, sit under the tree to watch the birds.

▶ A FEW DRY-LAID FLAGSTONES edged by golden creeping Jenny and creeping thyme make this patio look like a natural part of the surrounding garden. When the thyme is stepped on, it releases a sweet fragrance.

◄ A COUPLE OF CHAIRS, an occasional table, and an umbrella create a casual seating area on a corner of this lawn. The furniture is sturdy enough so it won't blow over on windy days yet light enough to be moved when the lawn is mowed.

▶ THIS SMALL SEATING AREA is tucked into a corner of the garden. It measures just 5 ft. wide, but it is large enough for a café table and two chairs, creating a quiet spot to enjoy an afternoon cup of tea, write a letter, or take a short lunch break.

◄ A TREE WITH A BROAD canopy of leaves offers a shady seating area along the loosely defined edge of this backyard. The heavy, rustic-style table and benches blend in with their surroundings. Cushions make the seating more comfortable.

▶ A SWING HANGING FROM A TREE, an arbor, or a porch will create a romantic seating area for two. Leave a few feet of unobstructed space in front of and behind the swing to allow for movement. For stability, a swing needs to be anchored by sturdy supports.

▼ THE ADDITION OF A HAMMOCK in the backyard provides a spot to nap. It is also a fun piece of outdoor furniture that will occupy children for hours. String it between two trees or mount it on sturdy posts.

▲ THE PERFECT SPOT for an afternoon nap, this outdoor bed also provides a colorful accent to the garden. A plastic, zippered mattress bag protects the mattress during an unexpected shower. Quick-drying fabrics designed for outdoor use will resist fading from prolonged sun exposure.

Council Rings
with a Modern Twist

COUNCIL RINGS CONJURE UP MEMORIES—campers gathered in a circle around a campfire to sing songs, tell stories, and roast marshmallows. Although the origins of council rings are rooted in Viking and Native American traditions, noted 20th-century landscape architect Jens Jensen is credited with the modern version of the council ring. His signature design features circular seating walls made of native stone, often placed in woodland clearings.

A council ring is a magical gathering space in the landscape, especially on a secluded mountain property or in a rustic retreat. A simple council ring can be created with a circle of boulders or tree stumps. Or it can be as elaborate as an artfully crafted stone seating wall surrounding a flagstone patio with a fire pit. If a ring in the woods includes a fire pit, make sure the spot is cleared both overhead and around the edges to prevent the chance of spreading fires.

▲ COUNCIL RINGS of the early 20th century inspired the design of this contemporary outdoor meditation area in the woods. The area has a circular layout, a small water feature, and a stone seating wall that defines the space.

◀ NATURAL MATERIALS such as logs, large tree stumps, and slabs of stone can be converted into garden benches. This bench, crafted from a granite slab held up by two boulders, looks as if it has always been a part of the landscape.

Lighting the Outdoors

IF YOU ARE GOING TO UNWIND, COOK, AND ENTERTAIN OUTDOORS AFTER DARK, you'll need to see what you are doing. Fortunately, there are more practical and aesthetic options than the glare of a floodlight. Downlights placed high on walls, under eaves, or in trees illuminate seating, dining, and recreational areas, while path and step lights allow you to move about safely and with ease. Tabletop and task lights make it possible to see what's cooking in the outdoor kitchen.

Outdoor lighting is also used to create ambience. Uplights accent trees, while spotlights call attention to architectural elements or decorative objects in the landscape; both cast intriguing shadows on nearby walls. Tea lights, torches, and candles all help set a festive or romantic mood. By mixing and matching different types of lighting, you can achieve a dramatic light show or a subtle glow in the yard.

▲ OUTDOOR LIGHTING FIXTURES come in a wide range of styles to match almost any home decor. This Oriental-style lantern hangs from a low copper post. It lights paths and low plantings but stands on its own as a decorative element.

▲ ACCENT LIGHTING calls attention to form and pattern in a landscape. This unusual structure is a recirculating water feature with water flowing from a broad shower head. A single light shines into the streaming water and calls attention to the pattern of the tower's construction.

◄ THIS GRANITE LIGHT FIXTURE illuminates a stepping-stone path through a backyard. The sturdy stone post surrounds the bulbs and wiring. The frosted-glass windows produce a soft glow that extends to the ground.

▼LIGHTS THAT IMPROVE safety are important elements in a backyard. These path lights highlight steps along a woodland path. The light-colored edging on the steps makes it easier to see the grade changes in low light.

▲ LAYERS OF LIGHTING transform this deck into a dramatic space. Uplights mounted on the deck and in the trees highlight playful branching patterns. Downlights mounted on the house wash over the deck to provide overall lighting, and candles add a romantic ambience for dining.

◀ STYLISH LAMPS have been introduced for outdoor use. This floor lamp and companion table lamp feature woven-resin, wicker-style frames, water- and fade-resistant fabric shades, and solid bases that stay stable and upright on windy days.

Understanding Low-Voltage Lighting

LOW-VOLTAGE LIGHTING runs at only 12 volts, making it safe to install yourself. To illuminate a path or small patio, a kit with several fixtures, cable, and a transformer (which plugs into a GFIC-rated outlet to convert household current) may suit your needs. For larger areas or complex lighting schemes, buy fixtures a la carte and choose a transformer that can handle slightly more wattage than your fixtures require (add up the total watts) for potential expansion. Once the cable and fixtures have been laid out, test the lights and make desired adjustments. Finally, bury the cable in a 5-in. trench for protection.

▲ CORDLESS TABLE LAMPS are convenient to use in areas where there are no outlets. This lamp is waterproof, features a dimmer control, and runs for up to eight hours on a single battery charge.

▶ MULTIPLE LIGHTS create exciting outdoor rooms. This space features underwater lights to emphasize the fountain so it can be viewed from both indoors and out. Downlights illuminate the patio and plantings; uplights accent the trees. A wall sconce near the back door was added for safety.

A SPOTLIGHT has a narrower, more precise beam than a flood-light and is an appropriate choice of lighting when accenting sculpture, plants, and architectural elements. To vary the effects a spotlight makes, mount it on the ground (such as the light at the corner of the arbor), to one side, or from above a structure.

ILLUMINATING BOTH A SWIMMING POOL and the surrounding deck improves safety. Underwater spotlights, step lights, and fiber-optic lighting along the rim create a soft glow in this pool. Step lights, ceiling lights, and wall sconces mounted near the deck ensure safe footing around the pool.

Adding Ambience with Accent Lighting

ACCENT LIGHTING ENHANCES THE MOOD OUTDOORS while highlighting special elements in the landscape. Strategically positioned uplights, downlights, and spotlights can highlight the unique branching structure of a tree, cast interesting shadows on nearby walls or paving, emphasize the texture of a stone wall, call attention to the movement of plants in the slightest of breezes, and showcase a garden sculpture or water feature. Candles placed on a table or in a chandelier or torches placed around a pool will create a romantic atmosphere. Strands of tiny lights strung in trees evoke a festive mood. Mix and match several different types of lighting to make the nighttime landscape interesting.

INDOOR LIGHTS can cast a surprising amount of soft light on adjacent outdoor spaces. To enhance the interior lighting that spills out into this backyard, accent lights focused on water features, architectural structures, and plants all work together to bring the landscape to life.

▲ A SPOTLIGHT aimed at this Japanese maple casts a striking shadow on the nearby wall. To achieve a similar effect with a piece of outdoor sculpture, direct a spotlight at the object from one or both sides. Excess light also bounces softly back onto the surrounding patio.

◄ LOW-PROFILE, FLUSH-MOUNTED LIGHTS can be attached to deck railings and fitted with 20-watt bulbs to create a soft glow over the deck's surface. They are also a practical choice for illuminating steps.

Backyard Fun and Games

For the ultimate playground, look no farther than your own backyard. Lawns can be used for everything from a game of tag or touch football to badminton or croquet. Patios are the perfect spot for hopscotch, jump rope, and board games. Special areas can also be designated for swimming, play structures, or court games such as basketball or shuffleboard.

Include something for each member of the family in your plan. Start with play spaces for young children that are visible from indoors and out. Older children appreciate gathering places farther away from parental view, with ample room to run, hide, and explore. Teens often prefer group activities such as volleyball or soccer. And don't forget spaces the entire family can enjoy—perhaps a horseshoe pitch, badminton court, or swimming pool.

The backyard can evolve as your family grows, too. Consider the kinds of spaces that may better suit your family five to ten years from now and which ones you may outgrow. A lawn may be the perfect spot for a swimming pool, a playhouse could be converted into a potting shed, or a swing set might be replaced by a tetherball pole. Plan ahead, so changes will have minimal impact on the rest of your yard.

◄ AS CHILDREN GROW OLDER, they tend to prefer more complex play equipment and structures that are located farther from the house. This play structure, nestled on a distant patch of lawn surrounded by trees and shrubbery, is small but includes a lookout, slide, climbing wall, and sandbox.

Kids' Play Spaces

APLAYHOUSE, TREE HOUSE, OR PLAY STRUCTURE does more than just entertain children. It helps them to develop physically and socially and encourages them to think imaginatively. Design structures that will allow children to swing, climb, balance, slide, dream, and sit quietly in the backyard. Whether play structures are purchased from a store, built from a plan, or designed from scratch, they should be sturdy and free from splinters and rough edges.

Before installing equipment, select a site where young children can be easily observed at all times, and cover the playground with 8 in. to 12 in. of bark, sand, or pea gravel to create a safe, cushioned surface. Older children will appreciate a playhouse or tree house that affords greater privacy. A patch of lawn where young children can learn to walk and older children can play games is an important element of any backyard play space.

▼ A SMALL STONE PATIO was constructed near this play area as a convenient spot to relax while keeping an eye on youngsters. A dense evergreen hedge hugs the patio, creating a cozy seating area and screening the playground equipment from the street.

▲ THIS STURDY CEDAR PLAY STRUCTURE is just the right size for preschoolers. There are opportunities to climb and swing but never very high. The structure includes three swings, a rope and ladder for climbing, and a playhouse with an upper lookout (complete with telescope).

▶ CREATE SOFT LANDING SURFACES beneath and around play structures with 8 in. to 12 in. of bark mulch, washed pea gravel, or play sand. The sand in this play area offers a beach-like setting perfect for building sandcastles or playing with toy trucks.

Sandbox Options

BUILDING A SANDBOX **for young children is an easy afternoon do-it-yourself project. You can construct a 5-ft.-square, bottomless box with rot-resistant lumber (avoid timbers treated with creosote) or interlocking pavers and fill it with play sand. Another option is to design something more naturalistic—such as a sandpit bordered by smooth-surfaced, sitting-sized boulders or timber rounds—that blends into a woodland or garden setting. A sandbox can also be recessed into a brick or flagstone patio. Simply remove a section of pavers, dig out some of the soil, and replace it with sand.

Regardless of style, start with a gravel base for drainage. Add a sheet of landscape fabric to prevent earthworms from making their way up into the sand. Fill the box or area with 10 in. to 12 in. of play sand. (Unlike builders' sand, which will stain clothes, play sand has been filtered and cleaned.) Add a seat around the edge if the walls are not wide enough to sit on comfortably. And finish the project with a hinged, folding cover cut from marine-grade plywood or Plexiglas that will keep falling leaves and small animals out of the play space.

EASY SANDBOX DESIGNS

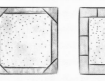
Wood frame

Interlocking pavers

Timber-round edge

Boulder edge

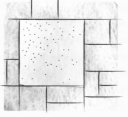
Recessed into patio

▼A SANDBOX AT LEAST 4 FT. SQUARE provides room for more than one child to play. This brightly colored sandbox extends from the garden wall. A broad ledge provides seating, and a hinged cover can be lowered when the sandbox is not in use.

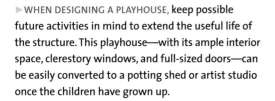
▶WHEN DESIGNING A PLAYHOUSE, keep possible future activities in mind to extend the useful life of the structure. This playhouse—with its ample interior space, clerestory windows, and full-sized doors—can be easily converted to a potting shed or artist studio once the children have grown up.

▲ THIS PAVED PATH circles the backyard, providing a smooth riding surface for tricycles and scooters. It surrounds a game lawn and leads to a play structure, a pint-sized picnic table, and a children's vegetable garden.

▶ THIS BACKYARD FEATURES a game court and brightly painted raised beds where children can plant and tend easy-to-grow vegetables such as radishes, lettuce, and corn. Both the game court and garden can be easily observed from indoors.

▲ STORE-BOUGHT PLAY STRUCTURES come in modular units with a wide range of add-on features that can be changed as kids grow. This structure includes swings, ladders, monkey bars, a slide, a tree house, and a picnic table.

◄ SWING SEATS come in several styles: molded safety seats for toddlers, soft rubber seats for older children, and tire swings, which can be hung either vertically or horizontally. The seats hang on chains for easy adjustment as children grow.

Playing It Safe

CHILDREN PUSH PLAY STRUCTURES to the limit. They'll swing as high as possible, climb on top of structures, and pack as many friends as they can into a fort or tree house. To keep structures safe, make sure they are built with solid materials, secure them with nuts and bolts, anchor them to the ground, and check them every few months. Kids also tend to run without looking ahead, so place structures away from steps, uneven surfaces, and tripping hazards. Position a swing so there's plenty of room to run around it without getting clunked in the head when the equipment is in use.

▲ BUILDING A PLAY STRUCTURE for older children near a shallow pond provides double the fun by attracting frogs, turtles, and butterflies. Kids access this tree house by climbing over a bridge and exit by sliding over the water.

◄ THIS FREESTANDING TREE HOUSE is built for adventure with a connecting bridge and tower. The hutlike design, combined with the surrounding plantings, makes the climbing structure feel as if it's in the middle of the jungle. The greenery also offers a bit of privacy for tree-house dwellers.

▲ THIS TREE HOUSE is a favorite neighborhood gathering spot for kids, and it's large enough to accommodate several friends at once. It offers open and private spaces and seating areas, plus bridges and ladders for climbing.

◄ A PLAY STRUCTURE MADE FROM WOOD blends into most residential landscapes. This structure has weathered to a natural gray that matches the siding on the house and complements the woodland setting.

Tree-House Innovation

A TREE HOUSE IS FOR CHILDREN and those who are children at heart. Most are built around a tree trunk or between several sturdy trees, but they may also be built out over sturdy branches, on stilts, or as freestanding structures on stilts. Use strong ropes to lash platforms to mature trees, and use screws to secure them to young trees (ropes will constrict a tree's growth over time). Better yet, build a self-supporting structure on posts around a tree to avoid potential tree damage.

Choose sturdy boards for floors and thinner boards for walls and roofs to keep the overall weight down. Build a broad deck or narrow balcony for lounging in the treetops, and add windows, skylights, or a greenhouse-style roof to brighten interior spaces. Both doors and hatches are appropriate in tree houses. Ladders, ropes, firehouse poles, slides, bridges, and climbing walls offer fun ways to come and go from a treetop retreat.

TREE-HOUSE DESIGNS

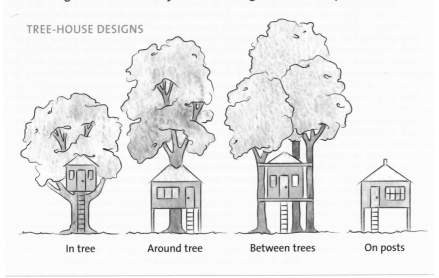

| In tree | Around tree | Between trees | On posts |

▲ TWO SWINGS are almost always better than one. It's more fun to swing with a companion, and a second seat will eliminate any squabbles over whose turn it is to swing. A flowering vine covers this swing frame, helping it blend into the landscape.

▲ALTHOUGH MOST TREE HOUSES are built in trees, this one sits atop a sturdy tree trunk that is just the right height for a viewing platform. The tree house is high enough to include a tire swing that hangs from the corner of the structure.

▶ KIDS LOVE PLAYING INSIDE TEEPEES. This one was built with bamboo poles and twine and planted with runner beans that will quickly form a shady, green cover. Hoop tunnels can be formed from willow stems and covered with fast-growing vines to create another fun play structure.

Backyard Bike Paths

Paved bike paths or dirt tracks are an easy addition to many backyards—especially those a quarter acre or more in size. Paths can follow the curve of a lawn, wind through the woods, circle the periphery, and even extend through the side and front yards. A path that is 3½ ft. to 4 ft. wide is ideal for bicycles, tricycles, scooters, and wagons. For safe and easy pedaling, paths should feature a smooth, compact surface such as packed granite fines or concrete, and they should make a complete loop or circle for continuous riding.

▲ LEAVE PLENTY OF SPACE—at least 5 ft. from an extended seat—in front of and behind swings, and avoid placing swings too close to pathways. This will give other children and adults room to safely pass by.

◄ PLAY STRUCTURES constructed from wood, painted natural colors, and surrounded with mulch can be placed unobtrusively in the landscape. This one is only a few feet high for safety purposes. Its low profile also helps it sit discreetly in a clearing among trees.

Recreational Spaces

BACKYARDS OF EVERY SIZE ARE SUITED TO RECREATIONAL ACTIVITIES and offer a convenient place to exercise, improve athletic skills, or simply have fun with friends. Sprawling suburban lawns are superbly suited for impromptu games of touch football, softball, and kick the can. Even in the tiniest of backyards, there's usually room to tuck in a tetherball set, putting green, or plunge pool.

Beyond physical space requirements, consider the characteristics and location of recreational areas. Games should be played on level ground that is free from rocks and roots for safety and enjoyment. They should also be played away from furniture, fireplaces, grills, and fragile plantings. Areas placed closest to the house will get more use, but activities that result in stray balls should be played away from windows. Consider designating areas along your property's periphery for paved, gravel, or grassy courts that may be used for basketball, bocce ball, horseshoes, or shuffleboard.

▲ A REGULATION-PLAY BOCCE COURT measures 13 ft. by 91 ft. but can be easily shortened for smaller spaces like this backyard. This court features a grassy playing surface, but compacted granite fines would work just as well.

◄ TENNIS COURTS, because of their size and tall, surrounding fences, can easily become obtrusive elements in the landscape. Evergreen hedges screen this tennis court, helping it blend in with the environment. A seating area beneath a hemlock tree offers a place to watch the game.

▶ HORSESHOES IS ONE OF THE FEW recreational activities suited to shade— as pools need lots of sun, balls need open space overhead, and running activities need a grassy surface. This horseshoe pitch was tucked into a woodland area defined by boulders and plantings.

◀ THIS OVERSIZED CHESS SET adds an element of surprise to the landscape and provides hours of playing fun. The 8-ft.-square board is a plastic mesh mat that snaps apart for portability, and the chess pieces are made from molded plastic.

The Home-Court Advantage

A HOME GAME COURT doesn't have to be regulation size. It can be slightly altered to fit available space in the backyard. General space guidelines for activities are:

Basketball: 30 ft. by 30 ft.

Tennis: 60 ft. by 120 ft.

Badminton: 27 ft. by 54 ft.

Volleyball: 42 ft. by 72 ft.

Croquet: 40 ft. by 50 ft.

Horseshoes: 50 ft. by 6 ft.

Shuffleboard: 52 ft. by 10 ft.

Boule: 40 ft. by 14 ft.

Bocce ball: 13 ft. by 76 ft.

Tetherball: 20 ft. in diameter

TETHERBALL COURT

Turf grass, dirt, or compacted gravel fines for surfaces

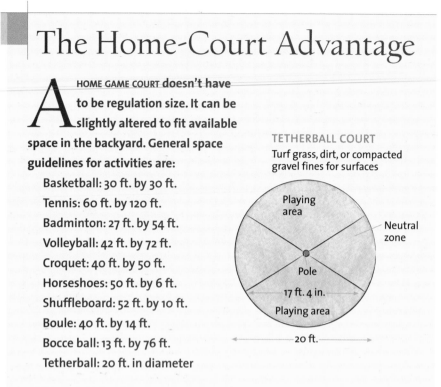

Playing area

Neutral zone

Pole

17 ft. 4 in.

Playing area

20 ft.

CROQUET COURT

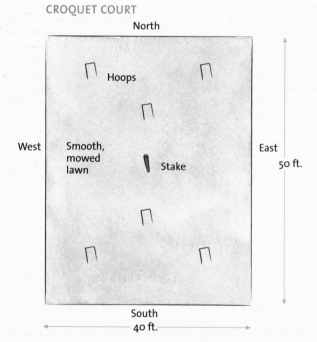

North

Hoops

West

Smooth, mowed lawn

Stake

East

50 ft.

South

40 ft.

BOCCE COURT

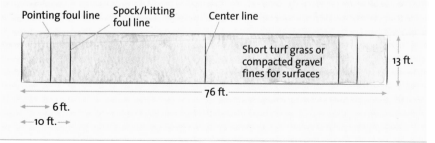

Pointing foul line

Spock/hitting foul line

Center line

Short turf grass or compacted gravel fines for surfaces

13 ft.

76 ft.

6 ft.

10 ft.

▲ CROQUET IS A FUN GAME for players of all ages, and it's an entertaining activity for casual outdoor parties. The game requires a smooth, level lawn, a croquet set, and a few enthusiastic players.

▲▲A TENNIS COURT NEEDS a tall
fence to contain loose balls.
Since it occupies so much space,
this tennis court was set along
the periphery of the yard.
A wildflower garden fills the
surrounding yard.

▶A HOME PUTTING GREEN
requires little space and can be
adapted to any lot shape. It features an easily maintained,
synthetic-turf surface that can
be installed by homeowners. The
perimeter of this green is put
to good use with a stone path,
seating area, and garden.

▲ A SMOOTH, LEVEL LAWN cleared of rocks and roots is the most adaptable surface for backyard recreation. For rough-and-tumble activities, choose a tough turf grass such as perennial ryegrass, tall fescue, or St. Augustine grass.

Defining a Play Area

A LAWN LOOKS ITS BEST with crisp, well-defined edges and a distinct shape—either geometric or broadly curving. Edging a lawn with brick or cut-stone cobbles keeps it neat and makes it easy to mow, but for safety reasons, they may not be a good choice for a rough-and-tumble play area. Instead, dig a shallow trench around the play area and fill it with mulch for a safe, attractive, and low-cost alternative. Select a grass that can withstand plenty of wear and tear. Mixtures of perennial ryegrass and tall fescues are the best choices for cool climates, while cultivars of St. Augustine grass are more suitable for warm climates.

▲ FOR HORSESHOES, sink two iron stakes in the ground 40 ft. apart. The stakes should extend approximately 15 in. aboveground, leaning slightly toward the opposite end of the court. Surround the stakes with shallow clay-, dirt-, or sand-filled pits edged with 2-ft. by 6-ft. timbers.

Pools and Spas

SWIMMING IS A FAVORITE AMERICAN PASTIME and a great way to get in shape. Of course, swimming is only half the fun of a backyard pool. A swimming pool is an ideal outdoor gathering space, especially when accompanied by a spacious pool deck, the shelter of an arbor or pool house, the convenience of an outdoor kitchen, and the warmth and ambience of an outdoor hearth.

Pools have changed dramatically in recent years. More shapes, sizes, styles, and special features are available than ever before—from pint-sized plunge pools to long lap pools to naturalistic pools anchored by boulders. Waterfalls, vanishing edges, and fiber-optic lighting add drama to a poolside setting, while wading areas, underwater benches, and spas make pools a great place to relax. Even without the extra features, there's nothing like a shimmering pool of water in the backyard for cooling off on a blistering hot summer day.

▶ A LAP POOL is a favorite choice for exercise. To establish a comfortable swimming pace and make flip turns, the pool should be at least 40 ft. long, 8 ft. wide, and 4 ft. deep. Wider pools, such as this one, easily accommodate other recreational activities.

▲A POOL CAN BE DESIGNED in any shape, size, or style imaginable. This naturalistic pool was designed to look more like a pond and features a sandy beach at one end. Boulders, streams, and waterfalls are other common additions to naturalistic pools.

▶THIS SMALL, SQUARE POOL is designed to blend into the garden. It is highlighted by a formal wall fountain on one end, is cleverly integrated into a tiered patio, and is surrounded by planters and raised beds.

▲ THE STONE SURROUNDING THIS POOL is echoed in the edging around garden beds, establishing a strong sense of unity throughout the landscape. Lawn and plantings come all the way up to the pool's edge, creating a naturalistic setting.

▶ STEPS MADE WITH A NONSLIP SURFACE provide safe and easy access to a pool. Well-designed, spacious steps can also provide a place to sit along the water's edge. These steps accentuate the curves of the pool and deck.

▲ THE DESIGN OF A POOLSIDE STRUCTURE is as important as the design of the pool. A well-thought out structure can create a feeling of enclosure, establish a sense of style, add a vertical element to a horizontal landscape, and provide necessary shade around the pool.

◄ A DARK INTERIOR POOL FINISH suits a naturalistic pool that is designed to look like a pond. Dark blue (shown here) and dark gray look natural and create excellent reflections yet still allow good visibility to the pool's bottom.

Popular Water Features

NEW SWIMMING POOL DESIGNS often include one or more water features. Falling water is the most popular, and it comes in many forms, from naturalistic streams and waterfalls to spouts, flumes, cascades, and sheet waterfalls. Another dramatic form of falling water is the vanishing edge, in which one or more sides of a pool seem to disappear as the water spills over its edge into a basin below. Fountains are also popular and come in a variety of spray patterns. Powerful underwater jets can transform a shallow seating area or underwater bench in your pool into a relaxing, spa-like gathering space.

▲ TO EXTEND THE SWIMMING SEASON, place a pool in full sun. The sun will warm the water earlier in spring and help keep temperatures comfortable into fall. This pool receives sun all day long, yet swimmers can escape to a nearby porch for relief from summer heat.

▲ THE BRIGHTLY COLORED MOSAIC TILES and contemporary styling of this water feature make it the focal point of a Florida backyard. The soothing sound that emanates from the sheet waterfall helps create a relaxing atmosphere around the pool.

▲ A LARGE, PROTRUDING BOULDER
looks at home in this naturalistic
pool and provides a gathering
area for swimmers. A swim-up
bar with seating is another way
for swimmers to congregate
while keeping cool.

◄ THE LARGE "JUMP ROCK" on the
side of this pool replaces a more
traditional diving board and
helps tie the pool to the surrounding boulder-strewn garden.
A small stone patio is positioned
on the hillside for enjoying both
the pool and garden.

▶THE RAISED SPA in this pool includes several water features. It has an infinity edge with water spilling into the pool below, a fountain that can be turned on when the spa is not in use, and four water spouts along the exterior wall of the spa.

▼TO CREATE A WATERFALL, position a pool near a natural hillside, create a mound from soil excavated during pool construction, or build a raised spa with a dropped edge (like this one) several feet above the pool level.

▶NIGHTTIME IS A ROMANTIC TIME around a pool, but good visibility is still essential. This pool features underwater lights and deck lights to illuminate the area for safety. The white pool steps are edged with small blue tiles to improve visibility during night and daytime.

Vanishing-Edge Pools

ONE OF THE MOST DRAMATIC ELEMENTS in modern swimming pool design is the infinity, negative, or vanishing edge in which a rim of the pool is dropped to allow water to flow over it. The water falls into a catch basin and recirculates into the pool. When viewed from above, the water appears to vanish over the pool's edge. The drama of a vanishing edge calls attention to the views beyond the pool— whether rolling hills, woodland groves, or colorful gardens. When the dropped edge overlooks a lake or an ocean, the bodies of water appear to merge.

Viewed from below, that same dropped edge transforms the still surface of the pool into a cascading or tumbling water feature. Both the distance the water falls and the surface over which it falls affect its rhythmic sound. The wall may be straight, sloped, or staggered and can be finished with smooth masonry, colorful tile, or small pebbles to complement the surrounding architecture.

▲ THIS VANISHING-EDGE POOL is positioned so that it can be enjoyed as a formal, cascading water feature from the house and lawn. From the pool deck and garden above, it appears as a quiet reflecting pool.

◄ A PORTABLE SPA can be placed on a patio, deck, or porch. This spa, discreetly tucked into a corner of the patio, is surrounded by greenery and is accessible from both the upper and lower portions of the terrace.

▼ A SPA PLACED CLOSE TO THE HOUSE, like this one near the back door, will be used more frequently throughout the year. The closer the spa is to the house, the shorter the distance to and from the water on chilly days.

THE WATERLINE OF A SPA AND POOL (often referred to as the "scum line") can be difficult to keep clean. Adding ceramic tile around the edge of the pool makes cleaning easier. Here, it also adds a decorative element to the pool.

THIS SPA IS BUILT on the ground, so there was no need to provide added support for the weight of the unit. Its position below the deck railing provides seclusion and integrates it into the deck.

THE BROAD LEDGE around this raised spa provides a place to set down towels and drinks while relaxing in the water. Since the spa is about 15 in. above the ground, the ledge is just the right height for additional poolside seating.

POOL HOUSES

▶ **THIS COLORFUL YURT** creates a festive poolside atmosphere. Yurts, which range in size from 12 ft. to 30 ft. in diameter, are constructed from stronger materials than those used for tents but utilize fewer materials than would a pool house. They can house a spa or be furnished like a pool house.

▼ **THIS BACKYARD AREA** is set up to extend the time spent outdoors. For sun-lovers, the area by the pool is unobstructed. As the hot afternoon sun beats down, though, the shaded area offers relief. An outdoor heater takes the chill off once the sun goes down.

◀ THE FOUR DOORS on this pool house fold back on hinges to allow sun and breezes into the structure. When a sudden shower rolls in, homeowners can seek shelter in the pool house, leaving the doors partially open for fresh air.

▼ WHEN A POOL IS LOCATED a distance away from the main house, a pool house is a convenient place for swimmers to dry off or change clothes before heading back to the house. A pool house can include a bathroom, kitchen, comfortable gathering spaces, and storage for pool equipment and towels.

Pool Storage Ideas

A SWIMMING POOL COMES WITH ASSORTED GEAR that needs to be stored nearby. The pool pump and filter should be placed within 100 ft. of the pool for operating efficiency—but away from your house and outdoor gathering areas to minimize noise. They may be enclosed in a ventilated shed or closet, placed behind an outbuilding, or screened from view with fences and plantings.

Store recreational gear in a nearby closet or shed. If you have a pool house, stash supplies in chests, drawers, or beneath skirted tables. Stack colorful dinnerware on open wall shelves, and fill decorative baskets, crates, and hampers with fresh towels.

OUTDOOR SHOWERS

▼AN OUTDOOR SHOWER is a refreshing way to rinse off after a swim. Teak weathers well outdoors, making it a handsome and natural choice for an outdoor shower floor and surrounds. Space floor planks so that water can flow into a drainage system beneath the deck.

▶AN OUTDOOR SHOWER can be located against the wall of a pool house, tool shed, or other outdoor structure. This one features a partial wall for bathing privacy, while a dense thicket of shrubs screens the entire building from neighboring properties.

▼PLACE A SMALL BENCH, or shelves and hooks, near an outdoor shower to hold wet and dry towels, a change of clothes, and other bathing amenities. A bath mat is also essential for drying wet feet.

▲THE OUTDOOR SHOWER and steel tub on this porch were designed for the pleasure of bathing and relaxing outdoors. They were built adjacent to the master bathroom for easy access to the home's plumbing.

▶THIS OUTDOOR SHOWER was designed and painted to match the home's contemporary architecture. An angled wall provides screening while allowing the bather to enjoy the scenic view. The nearby railing is a handy place to toss towels.

Specialty Gardens

OR SOME HOMEOWNERS, GARDENING IS A PASSION as important as entertaining or playing games. In fact, gardens are often the focal point of a backyard—as distinctive and dominant as any deck, patio, or swimming pool.

Gardens may be integrated in the landscape in any number of ways—as foundation plantings around the house and outbuildings, as mixed borders against fences or along paths, as island beds floating in a sea of lawn, as edible gardens just beyond the kitchen door, in containers on patios and decks, or as dense plantings that offer screening and privacy. These may be small, enclosed gardens or more expansive gardens that wrap around the periphery of a backyard, and they may be placed in sun or shade.

Landscaping elements such as fences, arbors, and paths give a garden structure, while decorative accents—from birdhouses and benches to outdoor sculpture and water features—help give it character.

▼ A VINE-DRAPED ARBOR frames the entry into a backyard garden of raised beds filled with a variety of vegetables, herbs, and edible flowers. Beyond the garden are several small henhouses where the homeowner gathers eggs each day.

◄ THIS SMALL AND ORDERLY GARDEN is the focal point of the backyard. The white fence with its unique birdhouse posts defines the garden, which is filled with cosmos, artemisia, thyme, basil, and nasturtiums and traversed on a stepping-stone path.

▲ NATURALLY ROT-RESISTANT locust branches make sturdy garden structures and furniture. This rustic arbor features a hanging swing, the perfect spot for a gardener to take a break from the day's gardening chores.

◄ THIS HEDGED CORRIDOR features a clipped boxwood parterre and a rustic pergola draped with climbing roses and other flowering vines. It serves as a formal, ornamental passageway amid a series of backyard garden rooms.

▲ A KITCHEN GARDEN suits even the most formal landscape. This one is designed like a traditional French potager, with separate beds devoted to different herbs and salad greens. The beds with trellises support climbing and rambling vegetables such as squash, beans, peppers, and tomatoes.

▶ RAISED BEDS provide better drainage and are easier to access than in-ground gardens. The ledges of a bed can offer seating as well. Though beds are used most often to grow vegetables and herbs, they can also accommodate cutting gardens for flowers.

Edible Gardens

Nothing beats the flavor of home-grown vegetables or freshly picked herbs. A compact kitchen garden filled with colorful herbs, vegetables, and edible flowers can be conveniently located near the back door—where it can be quickly and easily reached while planning and cooking meals. Raised planting beds—which are built from stone, brick, boards, or timbers and filled with improved soil to increase plant production—are attractive and can be more easily tended than in-ground beds. Sprawling vegetables, such as squash, tomatoes, and beans, can be grown in cages or trained up trellises and garden teepees to maximize space. The growing season can be extended by using protective plant covers such as glass cloches (bell jars), plastic and synthetic-cloth row covers, or portable cold frames.

▲ ALTHOUGH IT'S A SMALL PLOT, this charming country garden is framed by a handcrafted stick fence and filled with old-fashioned flowers, vegetables, and herbs. A rustic garden shed was built nearby as a convenient place for tools.

▲ A KITCHEN GARDEN can be much more than a functional space. With decorative features, such as these homemade concrete pavers imbedded with bits of ceramic tile, it can add style and personality to a backyard.

Backyard Buildings

A backyard building can expand your living space outdoors, get the office out of the house, or store your overflow of tools, toys, and pool supplies. Small buildings—from potting sheds and firewood shelters to artists' studios and woodworking shops—come in all shapes, sizes, and styles. Some are strictly utilitarian; others are comfortably furnished, with access to utilities, making them destinations for everyday activities. Buildings can be purchased as ready-to-assemble kits, created from a set of plans, or designed and built from scratch.

An outbuilding can be the focal point of the backyard, thoughtfully designed to complement a home's architecture and positioned to catch the eye. Likewise, a backyard structure can be painted a dark color or screened with plantings so that it recedes into the landscape.

When selecting a location for a backyard structure, consider its accessibility, exposure to the sun, and proximity to utilities. A firewood shelter should be built close to the house, a potting shed should be near the garden, and a retreat can be placed along the property's periphery. Adding a path from the house makes a backyard building easier to reach, especially during inclement weather. To accommodate wheelbarrows, carts, and mowers, make paths at least 4 ft. wide.

◄ BACKYARD RETREATS are often designed around a specific theme. This gardener's retreat is a casual, light-filled space decorated with rustic finds from antique stores and flea markets. The sunny window provides an ideal spot for growing herbs and getting seedlings off to a good start.

Studios and Retreats

KIDS LOVE FORTS, PLAYHOUSES, AND TREE HOUSES. Adults are similarly drawn to backyard retreats—cozy outbuildings for painting, writing, reading a good book, or relaxing with a cup of coffee. These are personal spaces designed for escaping the stresses of day-to-day living.

Some homeowners transform existing garages, playhouses, or sheds into inviting and functional spaces. For others, designing and building a retreat from scratch can be just as much fun as spending time in it later. Even the most rustic backyard retreat can be enjoyed during warmer seasons when there's good weather and natural light. Equipped with some of the luxuries of home—such as comfortable furnishings, a half-bath, and utilities—it can serve as a guesthouse, home office, or relaxing year-round refuge.

▼THIS WOOD-AND-STONE DINING PAVILION is the hub of the backyard and a destination for many gatherings. The canvas canopy provides shade and cover from light rain, while the fireplace adds warmth on cool evenings. Storage for firewood is built conveniently into adjacent walls.

▼ WHEN AN OUTBUILDING PLAYS a dominant role in the backyard, details provide personality. This colonial-style building features a cantilevered roof with cedar-shake shingles, board shutters with wrought-iron shutter dogs, and a brick foundation. It doubles as a potting shed and children's playhouse.

▲ A LANDSCAPE ARCHITECT converted his one-car garage into a home office and studio that anchors one end of the small backyard courtyard. A pergola runs along the front of the studio, providing a shady outdoor seating area next to a water feature.

▼ WHAT THIS WRITER'S STUDIO lacks in size and amenities it more than makes up for in style with natural timbers, weathered siding, and a stone stoop. Quiet places without distractions such as telephones and radios are exactly what many writers desire in a backyard studio.

▲ THIS BUILT-IN DESK FEATURES a long work surface and handy shelving for supplies. The old-fashioned typewriter can be put aside to make room for a laptop computer when it's time for serious writing. A view to the water and personal mementos provide inspiration.

◄ WINDOWS ARE ESSENTIAL in backyard retreats that lack electricity. These windows provide ample natural light and fresh, salt-air breezes for the writer. The small stained-glass window tucked into one corner of the far wall adds personality to the space.

Before You Build

BEFORE YOU BREAK GROUND FOR A BACKYARD OUTBUILDING, make sure your plans comply with local building codes, ordinances, and deed restrictions. If your project requires grading or running power, gas, telephone, or water lines to the outbuilding, you will probably need building permits and inspections. Find out if there are issues regarding public rights-of-way, property setbacks, structure height standards, or environmental sensitivities (such as wetland areas). Local officials, architects, landscape architects, builders, and engineering professionals familiar with local building codes can help you obtain appropriate permits and approvals.

▼OUTDOOR RETREATS are great places to use materials creatively. This rustic, Finnish-style sauna is housed in a log-cabin structure with a roof shingled with thin flagstone. The carved door and door frame have been brightly painted to contrast with the natural building materials.

▲ THIS GARDEN HOUSE FEATURES a distinctive Japanese-style design. Paneled-glass sliding doors and skylights along the roof's ridge fill the structure with natural light. The doors also allow the space to be opened up to the outdoors.

▶ INSIDE THE GARDEN HOUSE, storage and work spaces have been cleverly screened behind folding doors, allowing the homeowners to close off supplies, a large-basin sink, and flower-arranging works-in-progress when hosting other activities.

▲THIS ARTIST'S STUDIO in Maine is located in a historic neighborhood, so it was carefully designed to match the local architecture. Although it looks like a structure original to the site, it was recently constructed.

▲SLATE FROM RECYCLED SCHOOL BLACKBOARDS was purchased at a salvage yard and used to cover this sauna. A bridge with hand-cut and bark-stripped timber railings provides easy passage over rough terrain to this woodland retreat.

TUCKED INTO A SWEEPING BORDER that surrounds the lawn, this brightly painted shed serves as the primary focus of the garden. It has been landscaped much like a house, surrounded by foundation plantings and accented with a window box.

A PORTABLE SPA is transformed into a secluded, relaxing retreat when wood posts, bamboo fencing, and lush container plantings surround it. Architectural accents and pots with an Asian flair give the setting a distinct character.

▲ GET CREATIVE with storage in a backyard retreat. Unusual pieces of furniture, bins, crates, baskets, and buckets can be filled with tools, supplies, and collectible items. The space above the rafters can be converted into storage for less-frequently-used or hard-to-store items.

▲ A FLAGSTONE PATH leads to this garden cottage, making it the highlight of the backyard.
In addition to serving as a garden feature, this small building includes an outdoor seating
area. An abundance of windows allows natural light to flood the interior.

Designing a Studio

F OR SOME ARTISTS, WRITERS, AND CRAFTSPEOPLE, the backyard studio is their primary place of work. For others, it's a seasonal working space that offers a welcome change of pace.

While some people want their surroundings filled with personal effects, others prefer a spare, uncluttered space without distractions. To create a bright studio filled with natural light, install large windows and skylights. Add built-in or free-standing tables, desks, easels, or workbenches to create generous work surfaces. Use baskets, crates, and wall ledges to store small tools and materials, while reserving furniture and cabinetry for larger objects. Most important, include a comfortable seating area where you can indulge in a little dreaming.

◄ THIS RETREAT, built above a stone patio, blends a Japanese teahouse concept with Craftsman–style architecture. The structure features two large, sliding barn doors, a small sitting room with a fireplace, and an upstairs loft with a mattress.

Greenhouses and Potting Sheds

ANYONE WHO SPENDS TIME GARDENING OR TENDING A LAWN appreciates a dedicated work space—whether it's used for sharpening tools, starting seedlings, or hanging the water hose. Although greenhouses traditionally are for growing plants and potting sheds are for potting up seedlings and storing tools, the lines between the two are often blurred. It's not unusual to find a potting bench in a greenhouse or a sunny, plant-filled windowsill in a potting shed.

Just as often, these two spaces are connected or built close together—and never far from the garden. Greenhouses are bright, humid spaces used for protecting tender plants over winter, propagating new plants, and growing a wider range of plants than possible in a garden. They should be positioned for maximum sun exposure and away from trees to avoid falling branches. Both greenhouses and potting sheds benefit from access to water, whether provided by a spigot or a sink.

◄ BY USING SMALL WINDOWS in this shed, interior wall space is freed up for shelving, potting benches, and hanging tools, while supplemental lighting improves visibility on overcast days and during evenings. For buildings without electricity, rechargeable, battery-powered lamps or lanterns are affordable lighting options.

▼ ALTHOUGH THE HERBS AND FLOWERS in this garden are at their peak of perfection, the extensive use of structures—such as the potting shed, fence, raised beds, and arbor—will make the garden attractive even in the off-season.

TOOLS, PLANT STAKES, TWINE, and fertilizers are just steps away when a potting shed is conveniently located in the middle of a garden. A nearby location means that containers can be easily potted up and set in place, and flowers can be carried into the shed to be immediately hung in the rafters to dry.

Choosing a Greenhouse

SIZE IS THE MOST IMPORTANT FACTOR to consider when choosing a greenhouse. Freestanding greenhouses are available as small as 6 ft. by 8 ft., but most gardeners find that a structure measuring at least 8 ft. by 10 ft. better accommodates plants and people. It's easier to grow into a larger greenhouse than it is to expand a greenhouse when you outgrow your space.

There are numerous styles of greenhouses. Freestanding rectangular or hexagonal greenhouses, lean-to–style greenhouses that attach to a house or garage, and portable greenhouses with just enough room for a few small plants are several choices. Roofs may be peaked, rounded, or domed. Doors may swing or slide open. And windows or roofs may open to improve ventilation.

Greenhouse frames come in a variety of materials. Painted wood is beautiful, but rot-resistant cedar and anodized or enamel-coated aluminum is much easier to maintain. Although most greenhouses still have glass panels, new UV-treated polycarbonate panels are more energy efficient and less susceptible to breakage. Pea gravel is a practical choice for greenhouse flooring. It won't become slick when wet and allows excess water to soak into the soil.

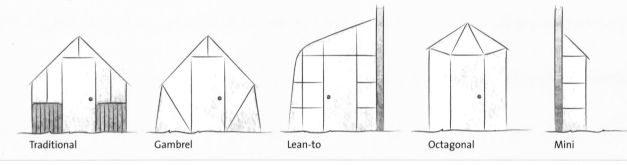

| Traditional | Gambrel | Lean-to | Octagonal | Mini |

▶ THIS GARDEN HOUSE FEATURES a shingled roof, but the many windows on each wall make it a bright place for over-wintering tender plants and growing houseplants during the summer. Inside, there's room to sit and enjoy the view and make notes in a garden journal.

A GREENHOUSE CAN BE BOTH decorative and functional. This Victorian-style greenhouse is the highlight of the garden, positioned at a bend in the path where you can't help but notice it as you move into the yard.

INSIDE THE GREENHOUSE, dry-laid brick floors allow excess water to soak into the ground, while a long counter affords plenty of space for starting seeds and potting up containers. Window shelves are lined with plants, while potting soil and supplies are stashed under the counter.

Warming a Greenhouse

GREENHOUSE HEATING REQUIREMENTS depend on what you are growing and where the structure is located. Cooler greenhouses are ideal for protecting frost-tender plants and growing cool-season vegetables. Warmer greenhouses are required for starting seedlings or growing tropical plants. Greenhouses in northern regions need a more reliable heat source than those in southern climates. Start by placing a greenhouse in an open, sunny area, with the longest side running east to west to maximize sun exposure. Several large barrels, filled with water and painted black, will absorb heat during the day and radiate that heat at night. Electric, oil, and gas heaters will provide additional warmth and more precise control over temperatures.

◄ A LATH HOUSE is a shaded structure used for hardening off tender seedlings or growing shade-loving plants like orchids and ferns. A lath house also provides a shaded holding area for nursery plants awaiting a permanent home in the garden.

▲ A GREENHOUSE is an ideal location for growing plants from seed. The benches, or tables, that hold flats and pots should drain easily after the plants are watered. They should also be sturdy enough to support pots filled with wet soil.

◄ A TRANSLUCENT ROOF allows enough light into this potting shed so that it doubles as an unheated greenhouse, sheltering tender plants from winter's cool weather. The top half of the barn-style door can be opened to improve ventilation.

A GREENHOUSE can be built against the south-facing wall of a house for convenient access, as well as for added protection against extreme temperature swings. The house wall shields the greenhouse from harsh northern winds and adds an insulating layer along one side.

Making Compost Convenient

COMPOST BINS AREN'T USUALLY THE MOST ATTRACTIVE GARDEN STRUCTURES, but to encourage their use, they must be conveniently located near the kitchen. So instead of looking at a pile of decaying leaves and vegetable peels, build an attractive wood or brick bin with a hinged lid that keeps the mess at bay and blends in with your home's architecture. As an alternative, screen less attractive but functional compost bins with an evergreen hedge, fence, or vine-draped trellis. A bin that holds approximately 1 cu. yd. (3 ft. wide by 3 ft. long by 3 ft. high) of materials is the most efficient at converting waste into rich compost.

WELL-WATERED PLANTS DRIP, so it's best to have a permeable greenhouse floor. A 2-in. to 4-in. layer of mulch (shown here), pea gravel, or crushed gravel will allow the water to drain and keep the floor from becoming slippery or muddy.

► LANDSCAPING HELPS PLAY DOWN the prominence of this large working greenhouse by providing a buffer of dense foliage with trees and shrubs. Including a few evergreens—such as junipers, cypress, laurels, or rhododendrons— increases year-round screening.

▼ ALTHOUGH POTTING AND GROWING ACTIVITIES can take place under the same roof, moving the potting bench to a separate location frees up additional space for plants in a greenhouse. This nearby potting shed also provides ample storage for tools, potting soils, and other gardening gear.

▲ THIS BACKYARD SHED IS DIVIDED into two sections. The front section, with a single door and windows, offers ample space for a workbench, as well as for storing tools and gear. The rear section, accessed through double doors, is for storing large power equipment.

Potting Shed Alternatives

IF YOU DON'T HAVE SPACE FOR A FREESTANDING SHED for potting up seedlings, stashing gardening tools, or storing pots in winter, simply improvise with what you do have. A garage or basement may have enough space for a table and shelves. A potting bench and hanging wall rack for tools can be tucked under the eaves of a house, garage, or other outbuilding. In a pinch, use an oversized wheelbarrow as a basin for mixing and storing custom potting soils. It can also serve as a portable workstation filled with gardening gear and rolled from one area to the next.

▼ THIS POTTING SHED FEATURES enclosed storage for tools, wheelbarrows, and power equipment. A potting bench and staging area are located beneath an attached shelter, part of which is covered in lattice. The lattice offers partial shade for acclimating plants started indoors or in a greenhouse.

▶ WITH ITS FRESH COAT of white paint, green roof shingles, and black shutters, this strategically placed potting shed is alluring. It's tucked into the woodland edge, just beyond a border, where it's a retreat as well as a place to take a break from gardening.

Storage Buildings

At the end of the day, there's rarely a shortage of toys, tools, bikes, hoses, ladders, or pool supplies to put away. Storage buildings can help keep things under control. A freestanding shed can be built from scratch or delivered to your property already assembled. Some are made from wood or metal; others are built from brick or stone. Choose materials that suit your budget and complement your home's architectural style.

An unused playhouse can often be adapted for reuse. If there's no room in your backyard for a freestanding storage shed, consider attaching a lean-to–style closet to your house or garage. There are other inexpensive options, too—mount a hanging rack for essential garden tools on an exterior wall near the back door, encase deck benches with lift-top seats, or enclose the space beneath your deck or porch with lattice to create convenient walk-in storage.

▲ INSTEAD OF A SHED, these homeowners built a row of waist-high, painted-wood storage cabinets along an exterior wall of their garage. The tops of the cabinets, which are protected by roof shingles, double as a holding area for recently purchased plants.

◄ A SMALL SECONDARY SHED is a good idea on larger properties with multiple or outlying gardens. This homeowner keeps an extra set of essential gardening tools in a refurbished outhouse to reduce the number of trips made to the main storage shed.

▲ FIREWOOD STORAGE should be conveniently located near the door with the easiest access to the fireplace. Well-seasoned firewood is rarely infested with bugs, but to be safe, don't store wood against your house for longer than a few weeks.

◄ WHEN SHEDS ARE DESIGNED to complement your house, they can be placed prominently in the landscape. This one features a hipped roofline and paneled double doors. The wide path both calls attention to the shed and improves access for mowers and wheelbarrows.

▼SPACE IS AT A PREMIUM in this small, in-town backyard. The owner designed an attractive peg rack for an exterior wall where garden tools can be hung and has arranged the tools so they add a sculptural accent to the garden.

◄IN THIS CLEVER DECK DESIGN, colorful box planters of varying heights filled with foliage plants help camouflage a cubbyhole used for storing a bicycle and toys. A shallow planting bed with a built-in drainage system sits atop the storage unit.

►THE OVERSIZED BARN-STYLE DOORS on this shed open wide, making it easy to move riding mowers, tractors, boats, trailers, and even outdoor furniture in and out of storage. An adjacent area, accessed through a standard doorway, provides space for a workbench and storage shelves.

Stretching Your Storage Space

NEARLY EVERY STORAGE SHED, GARAGE, POOL HOUSE, POTTING SHED, AND BACKYARD STUDIO can benefit from increased storage capacity. Here are some ideas for organizing your storage areas to better accommodate toys, recreational gear, garden tools, power equipment, and pool-cleaning supplies.

- Place items in stackable bins, and then label the bins.
- Group items by size, and adjust shelf height to eliminate wasted space.
- Hang under-shelf baskets on fixed shelves to make the most of in-between spaces.
- Divide drawer space with adjustable inserts so that contents can be organized.
- Build cabinets or shelves from the floor all the way to the ceiling.
- Lay boards across rafters to create out-of-the-way shelving.
- Install a grid system on walls to support hanging items.
- Build a fold-down worktable into wall shelving, and line the back with pegboard for hanging small tools.
- Install a pocket door that slides into the wall rather than taking up floor and wall space.
- Mount bicycles on wall racks, and hang canoes from the ceiling using ropes and pulleys.
- Store large power equipment in the center of a room so the walls are still accessible.

▲ STORAGE SHEDS such as this one are often built on a concrete slab or piers raised slightly above ground level, so a ramp is necessary for rolling large equipment and wheelbarrows in and out of storage.

MODULAR SHELVING

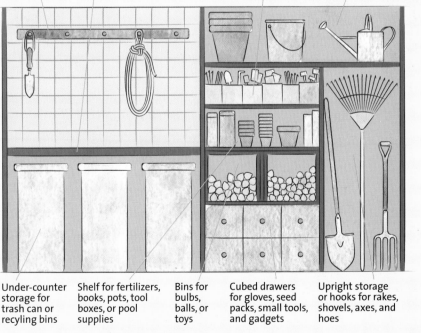

Peg rack with hooks for scissors, pliers, pruning shears, string, and wire

Built-in work counter

Small, upright boxes for hand tools, plant labels, pens, gadgets, and screws

Broad shelf for lightweight but bulky buckets and watering cans

Under-counter storage for trash can or recyling bins

Shelf for fertilizers, books, pots, tool boxes, or pool supplies

Bins for bulbs, balls, or toys

Cubed drawers for gloves, seed packs, small tools, and gadgets

Upright storage or hooks for rakes, shovels, axes, and hoes

▶ 'AMERICAN PILLAR' ROSES CLAMBER over a historic Nantucket shed and picket fence. Since roses aren't true climbers, they need the additional support of a trellis when grown against a building. The trellis also improves plant health by increasing air circulation around foliage.

▶ STORAGE SHEDS can be dressed up by training espaliered trees, climbing roses, or other vines along wire supports or trellises. On wooden structures, avoid vines that cling with aerial rootlets, such as ivy or climbing hydrangea, because they can damage the surface or work their way under shingles.

▼ A NARROW CEDAR SHED HOUSES the swimming-pool pump, filter, and cleaning supplies. It features two large doors that slide easily out of the way—a smart, space-saving feature. The shed screens the equipment from view and helps buffer noise generated by the pump.

◄ THIS EXTERIOR CLOSET provides an easily accessible place to stash heavy clay pots for the winter. Exterior closets may be part of the original design of a storage shed, potting shed, garage, or studio or later added as a lean-to structure.

▼ TRASH CANS CAN BE discreetly enclosed in a simple but attractive storage bin. This one is painted green so that it blends in with the landscape. Front-opening doors provide easy access when it's time to take the cans to the curb.

◄ FIREWOOD SHOULD BE STACKED under dry cover and seasoned for a year before use. This cedar-shingled firewood shelter features a large covered storage area, along with an uncovered, screened work area where firewood can be split.

Credits

CHAPTER 1

p. 4: Photo: © Brian Vanden Brink, Photographer 2004.

p. 5: Photo: © Lee Anne White, Design: Hermann Weiss, landscape architect.

p.6-7: (top) Photo: © www.davidduncan-livingston.com; (bottom) Photo: © Lee Anne White, Design: Louise Poer.

p. 8: (top) Photo: © Allan Mandell, Design: Jeff Glander; (bottom) Photo: © Tim Street-Porter, Design: Arthur Erickson, architect, and Barbara Barry, interior designer.

p. 9: (top) Photo: © www.davidduncan-livingston.com; (bottom) Photo: © Allan Mandell, Design: Linda Ernst.

p. 10: (top) Photo: © www.davidduncan-livingston.com; (bottom) Photo: © 2004 Samu Studios, Inc.

p. 11: Photo: © Alan & Linda Detrick, Design: Cording Landscape Design.

p. 12: (top) Photo: © Saxon Holt/ Photo Botanic, Design: Diana Stratton; (bottom) Photo: © Lee Anne White, Design: Sonny Garcia.

p. 13: Photo: Steve Silk © The Taunton Press, Inc., Design: Betty Ravenholt.

p. 14: (top) Photo: Charles Bickford © The Taunton Press, Inc., Design: David Sellers, Sellers and Company Architects; (bottom) Photo: © Tria Giovan.

p. 15: (top) Photo: Roe Osborn © The Taunton Press, Inc., Design: David D. Quillin, architect; (bottom) Photo: © Lee Anne White, Design: John Harper, Urban Earth.

CHAPTER 2

p. 16: Photo: © www.davidduncan-livingston.com.

p. 17: Photo: © Lee Anne White.

p. 18: (bottom) Photo: © Brian Vanden Brink, Photographer 2004, Design: Stephen Blatt, architect.

p. 19 (top) Photo: © Brian Vanden Brink, Photographer 2004, Design: Bullock & Company; (right) Photo: Charles Bickford © The Taunton Press, Inc., Design: Paul MacNeely, architect; (bottom) Photo: © Brian Vanden Brink, Photographer 2004, Design: Rob Whitten, architect.

p. 20: (top) Photo: © 2004 Samu Studios, Inc., Design: Bruce Nagle, AIA; (bottom) Photo: © Brian Vanden Brink, Photographer 2004, Design: Rob Whitten, architect.

p. 21: (left) Photo: © Tim Street-Porter; (top right) Photo © 2004 Samu Studios, Inc., Design: Luciana Samu; (bottom right) Photo: © Brian Vanden Brink, Photographer 2004, Design: Roc Caivano, architect.

p. 22: Kevin Ireton © The Taunton Press, Inc., Design: Cass Calder Smith, architect; (bottom) Photo: © 2004 Samu Studios, Inc., Design: Boccard/Suddell.

p. 23: Photos: © Brian Vanden Brink, Photographer 2004, Design: (left) Weather End Estate Furniture, (right bottom) Scholz & Barclay, architects.

p. 24: (left) Photo: © Lee Anne White, Design: Paula Refi, landscape designer; (top right) Photo: © 2004 Samu Studios, Inc., Design: Brian Shore, AIA; (bottom right) Photo: © Brian Vanden Brink, Photographer 2004, Design: John Gillespie, architect.

p. 25: (top) Photo: © Brian Vanden Brink, Photographer 2004; (bottom) Photo: © www.davidduncanlivingston.com.

p. 26: (top) Photo: Roe Osborn © The Taunton Press, Inc., Design: Laura Craft; (bottom) Photo: © www.davidduncan-livingston.com.

p. 27: (left) Photo: © www.davidduncan-livingston.com; (right) Photo: © Tim Street-Porter.

p. 28: (top) Photo and Design: courtesy of Richard McPherson, Landscape Architect, San Francisco; (bottom) Photo: Charles Bickford © The Taunton Press, Inc., Design: Adam Turner, Dovetail, Inc.

p. 29: Photo: Steve Silk © The Taunton Press, Inc.

p. 30: (left) Photo: © Brian Vanden Brink, Photographer 2004, Design: John Silverio; (right) Photo: © Brian Vanden Brink, Photographer 2004, Design: Weather End Estate Furniture.

p.31: Photos: © Brian Vanden Brink, Photographer 2004, Design: Rob Whitten, architect.

p.32 (top) Photo: © Brian Vanden Brink, Photographer 2004, Design: John Silverio; (bottom) Photo: © Saxon Holt/Photo Botanic.

p. 33: (top) Photo: © 2004 Samu Studios, Inc.; (bottom) Photo: © Lee Anne White, Design: Warren Simmonds, landscape architect.

p. 34: (top) Photo: © judywhite/GardenPhotos.com, Design: Nigel Boardman, Stephen Gelly & Jennifer Harkins; (bottom) Photo: © www.davidduncanlivingston.com.

p. 35: Photo: © 2004 Samu Studios, Inc., Design: Sherill Canet Design.

p. 36: (top) Photo: © www.davidduncan-livingston.com; (bottom) Photo: © Eric Roth.

p. 37: (top) Photo: © www.carolynbates.com, Design: Milford Cushman, Cushman & Beckstrom, Inc.; (bottom left) Photo: © Tria Giovan; (bottom right) Photo: © www.davidduncanlivingston.com.

p. 38: (left) Photo: © Brian Vanden Brink, Photographer 2004, Design: Elliott, Elliott, Norelius, architects; (right) Photo: © Brian Vanden Brink, Photographer 2004, Design: Sam Van Dam, architect.

p.39: Photo: © Brian Vanden Brink, Photographer 2004, Design: John Morris, architect.

p. 41: (top left) Photo: © Brian Vanden Brink, Photographer 2004, Design: Mark Hutker & Associates; (top right) Photo: © Tim Street-Porter, Design: Speigelman Interior Design; (bottom) Photo: © Lee Anne White.

p. 42: (top) Photo: © www.davidduncan-livingston.com; (bottom) Photo: © Brian Vanden Brink, Photographer 2004, Design: Lo Yi Chan.

p. 43: (top left) Photo: © Brian Vanden Brink, Photographer 2004, Design: Center-brook Architects; (top right) Photo: © Anne Gummerson Photography; (bottom left) Photo: © Brian Vanden Brink, Photographer 2004, Design: Weather End Estate Furniture; (bottom right) Photo: © Allan Mandell, Design: Lucy Hardiman.

p. 44: (left) Photo: © Allan Mandell, Design: Jeffrey Bale, landscape architect; (top right) Photo: © www.davidduncan-livingston.com; (bottom right) Photo: © Lee Anne White, Design: Hermann Weiss, landscape architect.

p. 45: Photo: © Tria Giovan.

p. 46: (top) Photo: © Lee Anne White; (bottom) Photo: © www.davidduncanlivingston.com.

p. 47: (top) Photo: © Lee Anne White, Design: Warren Simmonds, landscape architect; (bottom) Photo: © Lee Anne White, Design: Richard McPherson, Landscape Architect, San Francisco.

p.48: (top) Photo: © Lee Anne White; (bottom) Photo: © www.davidduncanlivingston.com.

p.49: (top) www.davidduncanlivingston.com, Design: David Yakish, landscape architect; (bottom) Photo: © Lee Anne White.

p. 50: (top left) www.davidduncanlivingston.com; (top right) Photo: © Alan & Linda Detrick, Design: Cording Landscape Design; (bottom left) Photo: © Alan & Linda Detrick; (bottom right) Photo: © Lee Anne White.

p. 51: Photo: © Alan & Linda Detrick, Design: Dean Riddle.

p. 52: (top) Photo and Design courtesy of Jeni Webber, landscape architect; (bottom) Photo: © Alan & Linda Detrick.

p. 53: (top) Photo: © www.carolynbates.com, Design: Birgit Deeds; (right top) Photo: © www.carolynbates. com, Design:Chris Dunn; (right bottom) Photo: © Saxon Holt/ Photo Botanic, Design: Cynthia Woodward.

p. 54: (left) Photo: © Lee Anne White; (right) Photo: © judywhite/GardenPhotos.com, Design: Guy Farthing.

p. 55: (top) Photo courtesy of Salsbury-Schweyer, Inc.; (bottom) Photo: © Lee Anne White.

p. 56: (top) Photo: © Lee Anne White, Design: Warren Simmonds, landscape architect; (bottom) Photo: © Lee Anne White, Design: Hermann Weiss, landscape architect.

p. 57: (top left) Photo: © Lee Anne White, Design: Dan Cleveland; (top right) Photo: © Lee Anne White, Design: Warren Simmonds, landscape architect; (bottom) Photo: © www.carolynbates.com, Design: Catherine Clemens, Clemens and Associates.

p. 58: (top left) Photo: © Brian Vanden Brink, Photographer 2004, Design: Horiuchi & Solien, landscape architects; (bottom left) Photo: © www.davidduncan-livingston.com; (right) Photo courtesy of Laneventure 2003.

p. 59 (top) Photo: © www.davidduncanlivingston.com; (bottom) Photo: © Allan Mandell, Design: Pamela Burton.

p. 60: (top) Photo: © Lee Anne White, Design: Jeni Webber, landscape architect; (bottom) Photo: © Tria Giovan.

p. 61: Photo: © Dency Kane.

p. 62: Photo: © Lee Anne White.

p. 63: Photo: © Saxon Holt/Photo Botanic.

p. 64: (left) Photo: © Tim Street-Porter, Design: Speigelman Interior Design; (right) Photo: Charles Miller © The Taunton Press, Inc., Design: Jon Stoumen, architect.

p. 65: (left) Photo: © Allan Mandell, Design: Michael Schultz; (right) Photo: © Tim Street-Porter, Design: Tichenor and Thorp, landscape architects.

p. 66: (top left) Photo: © Tria Giovan; (top right) Photo: © Lee Anne White; (bottom) Photo: © Anne Gummerson Photography.

p. 67: Photo: © Lee Anne White, Design: Sonny Garcia.

p. 68: Photo: © 2004 Samu Studios, Inc., Design: Andy Levtovsky.

p. 69: (top) Photo: © www.davidduncan-livingston.com; (bottom) Photo courtesy Richard McPherson, Landscape Architect, San Francisco.

p. 70: Photo courtesy Frontgate catalog.

p. 71: (top left) Photo: © Tim Street-Porter; (bottom left) Photo: © Eric Roth, Design: Bill Harris Architecture; (right) Photo: © www. carolynbates.com, Design: Catherine Clemens and Elizabeth Robechek, landscape architects, Clemens & Associates, Inc.

p. 72: (top left) Photo: © Jerry Pavia Photography, Inc.; (bottom left) Photo: © Lee Anne White, Landscape design: Beverley Ross/ Live in Color, Pool design: Leisure Living Pools; (right) Photo: © Robert Stein, Design: Barry Sugerman, architect.

p. 73: (top) Photo: © Robert Stein, Design: Barry Sugerman, architect; (bottom) Photo: © Lee Anne White.

p. 74: (left) Photo: © Deidra Walpole Photography, Design: Ruby Begonia Fine Gardens; (top right) Photo: © Deidra Walpole Photography, Design: Mark David Levine Design; (bottom right) Photo: © Deidra Walpole Photography, Design: Mayita Dinos Garden Design.

p. 75: Photo courtesy of Laneventure 2003.

p. 76: (top) Photo: © 2004 Samu Studios, Inc.; (bottom) Photo: © Tim Street-Porter, Design: Tichenor and Thorp, landscape architects.

p. 77: (top) Photo: © Tim Street-Porter; (bottom) Photo: © Tim Street-Porter.

p. 78: (top left) Photo: © Tim Street-Porter, Design: Dunas Landscape Architecture; (bottom left) Photo: © www.davidduncan-livingston.com; (right) Photo: © www.davidduncanlivingston.com.

p. 79: (top) Photo: © www.carolynbates.com, Design: Catherine Clemens, Clemens and Clemens Associates, Inc., Construction: Jess Clemens, Clemens and Associates, Inc.; (bottom) Photo: © www.davidduncanlivingston.com.

p. 80: (top) Photo: © www.carolynbates.com, Design and construction: Matt Furney, Firestone Landscaping; (bottom) Photo: © Dency Kane.

p. 81: (top left) Photo: © Deidra Walpole Photography, Design: New Leaf Garden Design; (bottom left) Photo: © Deidra Walpole Photography, Design: Green Scene; (top right) Photo courtesy of Laneventure 2003; (bottom right) Photo: © Deidra Walpole Photography, Design: Tony Miller/Scott Smith.

p. 82: (left) Photo: © Allan Mandell, Design: Lucy Hardiman; (right) Photo: © Allan Mandell, Design: Eryl Morton.

p. 83: Photo: © Lee Anne White, Design: David Bennet McMullin, garden designer.

p. 84: (left) Photo: © Allan Mandell, Design: Portland International Gardens; (right) Photo: © Allan Mandell, Design: Les Bugajski.

p. 85: (top left) Photo: © www.davidduncanlivingston.com; (bottom left) Photo: © 2004 Samu Studios, Inc., Design: Keller Sandren, AIA; (right) Photo: © Lee Anne White, Design: Ellis LanDesign.

p. 86: (top left) Photo: © Lee Anne White, Design: Michelle Derviss Landscapes Designed; (top right) Photo: Lee Anne White © The Taunton Press, Inc.; (bottom) Photo: © Tria Giovan.

p. 87: Photo: © Brian Vanden Brink, Photographer 2004, Design: Horiuchi & Solien, landscape architects.

p. 88: (top) Photo: © Robert Stein; (bottom) Photo: © 2004 Samu Studios, Inc.

p. 89: (top) Photo: © Alan & Linda Detrick; (bottom) Photo: © Tim Street-Porter, Design: Tichenor and Thorp, landscape architects.

p. 90: (left) Photo: © Jerry Pavia Photography, Inc.; (right) Photo: © Saxon Holt/PhotoBotanic, Design: Sally Robertson.

p. 91: (top) Photo: Saxon Holt/PhotoBotanic; (bottom) Photo courtesy of Salsbury-Schweyer, Inc.

p. 92: Photo: © Allan Mandell.

p. 93: (top) Photo: © www.davidduncanlivingston.com; (bottom) Photo: © Lee Anne White.

p. 94: (top left) Photo: © Lee Anne White; (top right) Photo: © Eric Roth; (bottom) Photo: © Allan Mandell.

p. 95: (top) Photo: © Lee Anne White, Design: Jeni Webber, landscape architect; (bottom) Photo: © Eric Roth.

p. 96: (left) Photo: © Jerry Pavia Photography, Inc.; (right) Photo: © Saxon Holt/PhotoBotanic.

p. 97: (top) Photo: © Brian Vanden Brink, Photographer 2004, Design: Horiuchi & Solien, landscape architects; (bottom) Photo: © Alan & Linda Detrick.

p. 98: (left) Photo: © Brian Vanden Brink, Photographer 2004, Design: Horiuchi & Solien, landscape architects; (center) Photo: Positive Images/Karen Bussolini, Design: John McKay; (right) Photo: © Alan & Linda Detrick.

p. 99: Photo: © Brian Vanden Brink, Photographer 2004.

p. 100: (top) Photo: © Kenneth Rice Photography/www.kenricephoto.com; Lighting Design: Randall Whitehead; (bottom) Photo courtesy Frontgage catalog.

p. 101: (top) Photo courtesy Frontgate catalog; (bottom) Photo: © Kenneth Rice Photography/www.kenricephoto.com, Builder: Renown Enterprises.

p. 102: (top) Photo: © Eric Roth; (bottom) Photo: © Kenneth Rice Photography/www.kenricephoto.com, Lighting design: Ruud Lighting.

p. 103: (top left) Photo: © Kenneth Rice Photography/www.kenricephoto.com, Lighting design: Janet Lennox Moyer, MSH Visual Planners; (top right) Photo: © Kenneth Rice Photography/www.kenricephoto.com, Lighting design: Janet Lennox Moyer, MSH Visual Planners; (bottom left) Photo: © Kenneth Rice Photography/ www.kenricephoto.com, Lighting design: Kichler Lighting.

CHAPTER 3

p. 104: Photo: © Dency Kane.

p. 105: Photo courtesy of Laneventure 2003.

p. 106: Photo: © Lee Anne White, Design: Betty Ajay.

p. 107: (top) Photo: © Kenneth Rice Photography/www.kenricephoto.com; (bottom) Photo: © Kenneth Rice Photography/www.kenricephoto.com.

p. 108: (left) Photo: © judywhite/GardenPhotos.com, Design: Jane Mooney, Installation: Hillier Landscapes; (right) Photo: © Saxon Holt/PhotoBotanic.

p. 109: (top) Photo: © Lee Anne White, Design: Michelle Derviss Landscapes Designed; (bottom) Photo: © judywhite/GardenPhotos.com.

p. 110: (top) Photo: © Lee Anne White, Landscape design: Don Dickerson, Inc.; (bottom) Photo: Liz Ball/Positive Images.

p. 111: (top) Photo: © judywhite/GardenPhotos.com, Design: David Stephens, Installation: Peter Dowle Plants & Gardens; (bottom) Photo: © Jerry Pavia Photography, Inc.

p. 112: Liz Ball/Positive Images.

p. 113: (left) Photo: © Saxon Holt/PhotoBotanic; (right) Photo: © Jerry Pavia Photography, Inc.

p. 114: (top) Photo: © www.carolynbates.com, Design: Pleasant Valley Landscaping; (bottom) Photo: © Saxon Holt/PhotoBotanic.

p. 115: (left) Photo: © Brian Vanden Brink, Photographer 2004, Design: Elliott Elliott, Norelius Architecture; (right) Photo: © Brian Vanden Brink, Photographer 2004, Design: Horiuchi & Solien, landscape architects.

p. 116: (left) Photo: © Lee Anne White, Design: Betty Ajay; (right) Photo: © Allan Mandell, Design: Ron Wagner & Nani Waddoups.

p. 117: (top) Photo: © Lee Anne White; (bottom) Photo: © judywhite/GardenPhotos.com, Design: Geoffrey Whiten.

p. 119: Photo: © www.carolynbates.com, Design: Barbara Van Raalte, Construction: Luanne Rotax.

p. 120: (top) Photo: © www.carolynbates.com, Design: Vincent and Allyson Bolduc; (bottom) Photo: © Deidra Walpole Photography, Design: Kennedy Landscape Design Associates.

p. 121: (top) Photo: © www.carolynbates.com, Design: Barbara Weedon Landscape Design; (bottom) Photo: © www.carolynbates.com, Styling: Caitrin Roesler.

p. 122: (top) Photo: © E. Andrew McKinney, Design: Jack Chandler & Associates, landscape architects; (bottom) Photo: © Robert Perron, Photographer.

p. 123: (top) Photo: © 2004 Samu Studios, Inc., Design: Bruce Nagel, AIA; (bottom) Photo: © Tim Street-Porter.

p. 124: (top) Photo: © Tim Street-Porter; (bottom) Photo: © Lee Anne White.

p. 125: Photo: © Lee Anne White, Design: Ellis LanDesign.

p. 126: (top left) Photo: © Alan & Linda Detrick, Design: Cording Landscape Design; (top right) Photo: © Eric Roth, Design: Nancy Smith; (bottom) Photo: © Alan & Linda Detrick, Design: Cording Landscape Design.

p. 127: (top) Photo: © www.carolynbates.com, Design: Keight Wagner, landscape architect; (bottom) Photo: © Eric Roth, Design: Bill Harris Architecture.

p. 128: (left) Photo: © Robert Stein, Design: Barry Sugerman, architect; (right) Photo: © www.carolynbates.com, Design and construction: Pleasant Valley Landscaping.

p. 129: (top) Photo: © Eric Roth, Design: © Alan & Linda Detrick, Design: Cording Landscape Design.

p. 130: (left) Photo: © Robert Stein, Design: Raymond Jungles, landscape architect; (top right) Photo: © Robert Stein, Design: Barry Sugerman, architect; (bottom right) Photo: © Barbara Bourne Photography, Design: London Pool & Spa, Inc.

p. 131: Photo: © Saxon Holt/PhotoBotanic.

p. 132: (top) Photo: © judywhite/GardenPhotos.com, Design: Geoffrey White; (bottom) Photo courtesy of Tony Benner Photography/Artistic Pools.

p. 133: (top) Photo: © Robert Stein, Design: Barry Sugerman, architect; (bottom left) Photo: © Robert Stein, Design: Barry Sugerman, architect; (bottom right) Photo: © www.carolynbates.com, Design: Michael Dugan, AIA, Construction: Tom Sheppard, Sheppard Custom Homes.

p. 134: (top) Photo: © Barbara Bourne Photography, Pool design: London Pool & Spa, Inc.; (bottom) Photo: © Alan Geller, San Francisco, Design: Michael McKay.

p. 135: (top) Photo: © www.carolynbates.com, Design: Keith Wagner, landscape architect; (bottom) Photo: © Eric Roth, Design: Bill Harris Architecture.

p. 136: (top) Photo: © Brian Vanden Brink, Photographer 2004, Design: Horiuchi & Solien, landscape architects; (bottom) Photo: © Eric Roth.

p. 137: (left) Photo: Kevin Ireton © The Taunton Press, Inc., Design: Cass Calder Smith, architect; (top right) Photo: © Eric Roth; (bottom right) Photo: Roe Osborn © The Taunton Press, Inc., Design: David R. Quillen, AIA.

p. 138: (left) Photo: © Brian Vanden Brink, Photographer 2004, Design: Ron Forest Fences; (right) Photo: © Lee Anne White.

p. 139: (top) Photo: © Lee Anne White, Design: Ellis LanDesign; (bottom) Photo: © Lee Anne White.

p. 140: (top left) Photo: © Tim Street-Porter; (top right) Photo: © Alan & Linda Detrick, Design: Dean Riddle; (bottom) Photo: © Saxon Holt/PhotoBotanic, Design: Diana Stratton.

p. 141: Photo: Lee Anne White © The Taunton Press, Inc.

CHAPTER 4

p. 142: Photo: © Eric Roth, Design: Polly Peters.

p. 143: Photo: © Jerry Pavia Photography, Inc.

p. 144: (bottom) Photo: © Brian Vanden Brink, Photographer 2004, Design: Sam Williamson, landscape architect; (top) Photo: © Allan Mandell, Design: Ron Wagner & Nani Waddoups.

p. 145: (left) Photo: © Allan Mandell, Design: Michael Schultz & Will Goodman; (right) Photo: © Lee Anne White.

p. 146: (top left) Photo: © Brian Vanden Brink, Photographer 2004, Design: South Mountain Builders; (top right) Photo: © Brian Vanden Brink, Photographer 2004, Design: South Mountain Builders;

(bottom) Photo: © Brian Vanden Brink, Photographer 2004, Design: South Mountain Builders.

p. 147: Photo: © Brian Vanden Brink, Photographer 2004.

p. 148: (top) Photo: © Brian Vanden Brink, Photographer 2004, Design: Carol Wilson, architect; (bottom) Photo: © Brian Vanden Brink, Photographer 2004, Design: Carol Wilson, architect.

p. 149: (left) Photo: Charles Bickford © The Taunton Press, Inc., Design: David Sellers, Sellers and Company Architects; (right) Photo: © Lee Anne White.

p. 150: (top) Photo: © 2004 Samu Studios, Inc., Design: Jim De Luca, AIA; (bottom) Photo: © Allan Mandell, Design: Jeffrey Bale.

p. 151: Photo: © Eric Roth, Design: Polly Peters.

p. 152: Photo: courtesy of John L. Harper.

p. 153: Photo: © Lee Anne White, Design: F. Malcom George, architect.

p. 154: (left) Photo: © Brian Vanden Brink, Photographer 2004, Design: Horiuchi & Solien, landscape architects; (right) Photo: © Brian Vanden Brink, Photographer 2004, Design: Horiuchi & Solien, landscape architects.

p. 155: Photo: © Brian Vanden Brink, Photographer 2004, Design: Horiuchi & Solien, landscape architects.

p. 156: Photo: © Brian Vanden Brink, Photographer 2004.

p. 157: (left) Photo: © Allan Mandell; (right) Photo: © Allan Mandell.

p. 158: (top left) Photo: © Tim Street-Porter; (top right) Photo: © Eric Roth; (bottom) Photo: © Tim Street-Porter, Design: Kathy Spitz, landscape architect.

p. 159: (top) Photo: © Tria Giovan; (bottom) Photo: © www.davidduncanlivingston.com.

p. 160: (top) Photo: © Eric Roth; (bottom left) Photo: © Alan & Linda Detrick; (bottom right) Photo: © Alan & Linda Detrick.

p. 161: (top) Photo: © Saxon Holt/PhotoBotanic; (bottom) Photo: © Alan & Linda Detrick.

p. 162: (left) Photo: Lee Anne White © The Taunton Press, Inc.; (left) Photo: © Allan Mandell, Design: Scott Kasterson.

p. 163: (top) Photo: © Brian Vanden Brink, Photographer 2004, Design: Scholz & Barclay, architects; (bottom) Photo: © Lee Anne White, Design: Mahan Rykiel Associates.

p. 164: (left) Photo: © Lee Anne White, Design: Hermann Weiss, landscape architect; (top right) Photo: © judywhite/GardenPhotos.com, Design: Natalie Charles; (bottom right) Photo: © Brian Vanden Brink, Photographer 2004, Design: Horiuchi & Solien, landscape architects.

p. 165: Photo: © Brian Vanden Brink, Photographer 2004, Design: Elliott, Elliott, Norelius Architecture.

p. 166: (top) Photo: © www.carolynbates.com; (bottom left) Photo: Karen Bussolini/Positive Images; (bottom right) Photo: © www.carolynbates.com.

p. 167: (top left) Photo: © Eric Roth; (top right) Photo: © Paula Refi; (bottom) photo: © Brian Vanden Brink, Photographer 2004, Design: John Silverio, architect.

Resources

Additional Reading

Architecture in the Garden by
James Van Sweden. Random
House, 2002.

*Fine Gardening Design Guides:
Landscaping Your Home.*
Taunton Books, 2001.

John Brookes Garden Masterclass
by John Brookes. Dorling
Kindersley, 2002.

*Taylor's Master Guide to Land-
scaping* by Rita Buchanan.
Houghton Mifflin, 2000.

The Essential Garden Book
by Terence Conran and Dan
Pearson. Crown Publishers,
Inc., 1998.

The Landscape Makeover Book
by Sara Jane von Trapp.
Taunton Books, 2000.

The Pool Idea Book by Lee Anne
White. Taunton Books, 2004.